IT'S ALL
TOO MUCH,
SO GET IT
TOGETHER

IT'S ALL TOO MUCH,
SO GET IT
TOGETHER

PETER WALSH

with illustrations by JOHN HENDRIX

SIMON & SCHUSTER BFYR

NEW YORK   LONDON   TORONTO   SYDNEY

SIMON & SCHUSTER BFYR
An imprint of Simon & Schuster Children's Publishing Division
1230 Avenue of the Americas, New York, New York 10020
Copyright © 2009 by Peter Walsh Design, Inc.
All rights reserved, including the right of reproduction in whole or in part in
any form.
SIMON & SCHUSTER BFYR is a trademark of Simon & Schuster, Inc.
For information about special discounts for bulk purchases, please
contact Simon & Schuster Special Sales at 1-866-506-1949 or
business@simonandschuster.com.
The Simon & Schuster Speakers Bureau can bring authors to your live
event. For more information or to book an event, contact the Simon
& Schuster Speakers Bureau at 1-866-248-3049 or visit our website
at www.simonspeakers.com.
Book design by Jane Archer/www.psbella.com
The text for this book is set in Social Gothic, Trade Gothic, and Clarendon.
The illustrations for this book are rendered in pen and ink.
Manufactured in the United States of America
10 9 8 7 6 5 4 3 2 1
Library of Congress Control Number 2009931666
ISBN 978-1-4169-9549-4

IT'S ALL TOO MUCH, SO GET IT TOGETHER

INTRODUCTION

A LIST OF WaYS YOU MIGHT HaVe ENDED UP WITH THIS BOOK

11. Your boyfriend got it for you as a "joke." Well, at least you *thought* it was a joke. . . .

10. Your girlfriend gave you that new graphic novel you really wanted, and you found this book tucked inside the same box. And when you pulled it out and were all, "Oh, what's this?" she opened her eyes *very wide* and said *very loudly,* "OH! WELL, HOW ON EARTH DID THAT GET IN THERE?"

9. You found it shoved into the glove compartment of your car on top of three broken ice scrapers and a crumpled-up McFlurry cup, with an anonymous note: *Thought you could maybe use this.*

8. Your best friend tossed it at you and said, "Dude, enough already!" You borrowed his favorite jacket eight months ago, and for the past eight months whenever he asks for it back, you just motion to that crazy pile-o'-clutter that was once your bedroom and say, "Well, I know it must be in here *somewhere.*"

7. Your dad came into your room wearing a raincoat and his old football helmet and said, "It's not safe to come in here without protection!" Then he put the book on your desk on top of those forty-five moldy music magazines from the eighties that you found at a garage sale. And ran away.

6. You woke up one morning and the book was under your pillow. There was glitter sprinkled around your bed, and your window was just ever-so-slightly open.

5. Your uncle got it for you as a "very early birthday present" (and your birthday is ten months away).

4. Your mom sent Woofie, the family dog, into your room carrying it in his mouth. She claimed Woofie bought it for you himself. But that just seems unlikely.

3. Whenever your older sister comes in your room, she pretends to be all upset and screams, "OH, NO! SOMEONE BROKE INTO YOUR ROOM AND RANSACKED IT!" and then says, "Oh wait, it's just like that." She gave you this book because she can no longer handle the stress of having to look at your mess.

2. You opened your closet and it just fell out on your head, along with that Best Nap Taker trophy you won in kindergarten and a half-deflated basketball. You have no idea where it came from. But then again, you don't know how half of that stuff got in there!

THEN again, maybe just maybe . . .

1. You're feeling totally overwhelmed by something in your life. Or many things in your life. Maybe you were wandering around the bookstore, and when you saw the bright yellow cover and the white text popping out at you screaming, *IT'S ALL TOO MUCH!* you wanted to high-five the book. Because you can so, *so* relate. (AND TRUST ME, IF YOU FEEL THAT WAY, YOU'RE NOT ALONE.)

Regardless of whether you got this book for yourself or whether you got it as a gift, chances are the fact that this book ended up in your hands means you probably have at least a little (and maybe even a very big) clutter problem. And maybe you are a little (or a lot) (or completely!) overwhelmed. And just maybe you could use some help getting organized.

People have lots of different thoughts and feelings when it comes to their clutter. Some are aware of their clutter. Some are *too* aware of their clutter. For some people their clutter is so overwhelming that they think it can't be dealt with. Or maybe it's so overwhelming that they can't bear to think about it at all! (I've known adults who were so overwhelmed by all the clutter they'd collected that they bought an ENTIRELY NEW HOUSE so that they would not have to clean up the first one. I am not even kidding!) Some people mistakenly think that only certain types of people can be organized, and that if they're not organized already, well, then there's no point in even trying!

But I am here to tell you that no matter how bad it is, no matter how unmanageable it seems, it can get done. It *will* get done. And when it gets done, your life will be profoundly changed for the better. And I can help.

But this book is about a lot more than just cleaning and about a lot more than just decluttering and about a lot more than just getting organized.

In fact, really, what this book is about is

you.

It's about who you are and who you want to be, what you want from your life and how you can best go about getting it. It's about you and your life and your stuff and how all of those things can work together more harmoniously. But more on that later. Much more on that later.

Some of the stuff that you're going to be asked to do on the pages that follow might feel like work. I won't lie. But I also promise it will be fun. I mean, maybe not winning-the-lottery fun, or being-crowned-prom-queen fun, or bungee-jumping fun (if you're into that sort of thing), but still . . . fun. (Besides, it'll definitely be better than taking a biology midterm, getting one of your teeth removed, hosting a party for twenty-five screaming five-year-olds, farting loudly in front of your entire class, farting quietly in front of someone you have a crush on, or bungee jumping [if you're scared of heights]). And unlike some of the stuff that you're supposed to learn in school that miiiight not seem like it's going to be super useful for the future, the stuff you're about to learn will actually help you for the rest of your life. *Starting right now . . .*

How do I know? Because I've gone into hundreds of people's homes—adults, kids, teens—and helped them change their lives. Make no mistake: I don't do it *for* them. I just give them the tools to do it themselves. I've seen their smiling faces, and I've heard the relief in their voices as they tell me how by doing things very similar to what you'll be taught to do in this book, their lives have been changed—they've gotten happier, their relationships have gotten better, they've felt more relaxed and less stressed, and they've been equipped to reach all the goals they have for their lives.

But first, back up. You're probably wondering who I am, and why exactly it is that so many people have let me come into their homes and let me poke around in their stuff. Not only let me, but invited me, and sometimes not only me but entire film crews, so that we could broadcast the most private bits of their homes on national TV. Why?

Well, that's a very good question. My name is Peter Walsh, and I'm a professional organizer.

I know to some of you that probably sounds like just about the worst job in the world, ranking just above dog-food taster and toenail clipper to the stars. But the thing is, I love my job. And it's not because I'm a freak for cleaning, but because I love helping people figure out what they want out of their lives and how they can go about getting it. I love showing people that buried under all the clutter in their homes is a better life waiting to be uncovered.

I've been a professional organizer for more than a decade. I had a show on the TLC network called *Clean Sweep*, in which I helped people declutter their lives. I regularly appear on *The Oprah Winfrey Show* and have a regular program on Oprah Radio. I'm a *New York Times* bestselling author, and I have written four organizational books in addition to the one you're reading right now, as well as a decluttering workbook. But I'm not telling you these things to brag. I'm telling you these things so that you believe me when I say that I have had a lot, I mean a *lot*, of decluttering experience.

I have gone into houses where there were tons, literally tons (as in *many thousands of pounds*), of extra crap cluttering the place up. And by the time I left, 100 percent of the junk (which equaled 90 percent of everything that was in the house!) had been removed. So no matter how overwhelming your own personal clutter might be, trust me that I've seen worse.

How did it get so bad? Why are so many people so cluttered? Well, a lot of reasons really. Some of which are complicated and one of which is awfully simple: Right now here in America we are all suffering from a terrible case of over-stuff-itization. To put it another way, we are all obsessed with **STUFF**.

Wanting **STUFF**, buying **STUFF**, getting **STUFF**, having **STUFF**, keeping **STUFF**.

But the thing is, we're so used to being obsessed with stuff, and so used to our friends, parents, and neighbors being obsessed with stuff too, that it's just become a way of life. And unless we stop and slow down and look very, very closely, it doesn't seem like an obsession at all. We don't even think about it or question it. It just seems normal, and we can't imagine it being any other way.

THINK aBOUT IT: When you're driving, walking, or riding the bus through your town, you pass a million different stores. And what are those stores selling? They're selling stuff. Then maybe you go over to a friend's house, and you open up a magazine. And what's in between articles? Ads for stuff! And maybe after that you and your friend sign onto the Internet, and hey, what's that banner flashing there at the top of the screen? Oh, wait, it's a little message telling us about more stuff we need. Then when you get home, you might turn on the TV, and at every commercial break people come onto the TV screen and tell you about all the amazing new products that you're missing out on and that you must go out and buy. Act now! Act fast! Before it's too late!

Why, sometimes even the shows themselves are all about the stuff you should buy. Like the one that comes on late at night where that guy tells you that you should definitely invest in some of his giant felt napkins, because they are just

so absorbent and are going to make your life easier and less liquidy. Or that one where the lady tells you all about how you must, you *must*, buy this special plastic tube in which a person can cook spaghetti very easily and quickly (since it's, y'know, so time-consuming and labor-intensive otherwise?).

STUFF, STUFF, **STUFF, STUFF, STUFF, STUFF, STUFF!**

Well, no wonder you might feel a little cluttered. It's no wonder so many of us do. Wherever we look, we are told that acquiring new stuff is going to make our lives easier, happier, more exciting, and more fun. That acquiring new stuff will make us smell better and look better, will make our skin softer and our hair shinier. That we will be perfectly in shape and smiling big, bright, white-toothed smiles all the time if we just buy the right combination of appropriate products that will help us achieve all of our goals. But it's not just about getting the right products; it's about buying the right number of products. And more is always, always better. If one TV is GOOD, then two TVs are BETTER. And if two TVs are GOOD, then two GIANT TVs are BETTER. MORE BIGGER. MORE BETTER. It's no surprise that we're running out of room!

But what happens when we find that we have too much stuff and begin to feel overwhelmed by it? We're told that if we just buy the right plastic boxes, or filing systems, or closet organizers, or special vacuum-bags that will enable us to pump the air out of our sweaters—or better yet a bigger closet in which to keep our sweaters!—then all our problems will be solved. And then we will all drift off into a magical dreamland where unicorns do our laundry and flying kittens make our beds. And we all live happily ever after.

The problem is that unicorns can't do laundry. Oh, yeah, and that *this dream is not reality.*

If having more stuff were the answer, then we'd all be thrilled already! There wouldn't be so many people suffering from anxiety and feeling overwhelmed by their clutter. But what if all the stuff is in fact *causing* some of the crazy problems we're trying to solve with it? What if the answer lies not in having more stuff, or even less stuff, but in having a different relationship with our stuff? What if the stuff *isn't even about the stuff*?

CONFUSED? CURIOUS? EXCITED? DUBIOUS?

Well then, let's get started. . . .

A QUICK BREAKDOWN OF THE BOOK YOU'RE ABOUT TO READ . . .

PART 1:

LET'S TALK ABOUT THE CLUTTER

In part 1 we'll jump right in and do a full-fledged clutter dissection! Some of the topics we'll cover are the clutter and how it's affecting your life, reasons to declutter, internal and external clutter, and some excuses people have for holding on to their clutter. We'll also discuss *the* most important question to ask yourself when it comes to decluttering (note, it has nothing to do with trash bags or plastic storage boxes!).

PART 2:

A STEP-BY-STEP GUIDE TO DECLUTTERING YOUR SPACE

In part 2 we get into the real nitty-gritty of the decluttering. This section includes all sorts of tips and tricks to make your decluttering easier, less stressful, and even fun. (No, I'm serious!) By the time you get through part 2, even the most overwhelming clutter situation won't seem so bad. This section also includes tips for staying clutter-free long after the last recycling bag has been taken to the curb.

PART 3:

APPLYING THESE SKILLS TO THE REST OF YOUR LIFE

Decluttering isn't just about cleaning up the mess; it's about looking at the *stuff* in a whole new way. And once you get used to looking at stuff in a new way, you can look at your entire *life* in a new way. The result? Less junk, a clearer mind, and a better life!

PART 1

LET'S TALK ABOUT THE CLUTTER

To most people, sophomore student Stephanie Scatterini seems like she has it all together. She's in three honors classes (chemistry, French, and English) and on two sports teams (JV field hockey in the fall, and track in the spring). She's on the yearbook committee and the homecoming committee and active in the Eco-Friends club. When she gets home from school or practice or meetings, she looks after her brother and sisters. On weekends she babysits for her neighbors' kids to earn extra money. Her parents want to make sure she goes to a really good college so she can become a lawyer like her mom, so she's enrolled in an SAT-prep class and a precollege law class at a local community college.

Stephanie knows she has to plan for her future. College is, after all, very important. And so she knows she needs to do as much as humanly possible to get into the best school. The problem is, her grades are starting to suffer, because she can never find time to study . . . let alone a *place* to study! Her room is so filled with all the crap she's collected and has had no time to go through that she often ends up trying to do her homework on the bathroom floor!

Stephanie always does her best to do all of her homework assignments on time, but sometimes she makes careless errors because she's not really able to concentrate very well. And on more than one occasion she's thought she forgot her homework at home, only later to find it crushed at the bottom of her locker under a pile of sports equipment, yearbook forms, and posters for the Eco-Friends' weekly bake sales.

The SAT class she's taking might be really helpful, but she's ended up having to miss it a couple of times because of scheduling conflicts. And now she's totally behind and has pretty much no idea what's going on in the class. Which makes her feel incredibly guilty, of course, because her parents are paying for the class, and it's expensive!

She's made it to a couple of the law classes, but she finds them completely uninteresting, because the truth is that Stephanie doesn't actually have any interest in becoming a lawyer. But she hasn't said anything; her parents are so set on it, and she hates to disappoint them. Actually, she hates disappointing anyone, but she feels like she's been doing it a lot lately. She's had to miss a few of her track meets because it seems like she has a cold every other week. She thinks it might be from stress and from the fact that she doesn't usually get much sleep.

On the outside Stephanie might look like she has it all together; on the inside she has it all together *squashed and jumbled into a big mess!* If you look in her backpack or her locker or the trunk of her car, you'll find a mass of clutter: a combination of schoolbooks, notes from homecoming committee meetings, printouts of possible yearbook photos, handouts from her law seminar, SAT books, field hockey equipment, deflated basketballs, random craft supplies she brings to the houses of the kids she babysits for, reusable water bottles, granola bar wrappers (she almost never has time to eat a real lunch), and . . . who even knows what else! And if you look in her bedroom . . . well. As Stephanie's best friend once put it, "It looks like a hurricane threw up in here."

Speaking of friends. Stephanie actually hasn't really gotten to spend any time with her best friend in more than a month. Or with any of her other friends either! And as for her romantic life . . . it's as nonexistent as her free time. There was a guy she had a crush on last year who seemed to like her too. He called her once and sent her two e-mails, but she never got home early enough to call him back. And her e-mail in-box was so full that she didn't even *notice* that he'd sent her anything until it was too late!

Sometimes late at night Stephanie will lie in her bed, unable to sleep, curled into a stomachache-y ball. The moonlight coming through her window will illuminate the piles and piles of stuff scattered all around her room, and she'll find herself reminded of all the things she needs to do the next day. And the things that she was supposed to do that day that she didn't have time for. And then she'll wonder exactly how she got into this mess. She'll wonder how she let her room get so cluttered, how she let her *life* get so cluttered. And she'll have no answer, so she'll just stare at the piles and piles and piles and wish and wish and wish that they'd get smaller somehow on their own.

But of course they never do.

When she finally does fall asleep, she often has a recurring nightmare in which all the piles in her room keep growing until they pop right through the roof.

CHAPTER 1

GETTING STARTED

It's all too much! Have you ever heard someone say that phrase before? You probably have. Maybe you've even said it yourself. Maybe you even said it when you picked up this book: *It's. All. Too. Much!*

This is not a phrase you say while smiling. You don't say it relaxing in the park with a good book, or sipping hot chocolate in front of a roaring fireplace, or playing Frisbee at the beach, or going to see your favorite band, or while having a barbecue in your backyard with your friends.

When you say this phrase, it's because you are *stressed.* You are rigid and you are tense. Your shoulders and neck and back hurt. Maybe you feel not-so-great in the stomach. When you say this phrase, your face gets all scrunched up. And maybe it turns red. And maybe you wave your hands around. And maybe your hair stands up on end and little curls of smoke come out of your ears. (Okay, this last one is only in cartoons . . . but you get the picture.)

"It's all too much!" is not a happy phrase. It is, however, a pretty expressive phrase, because it means so many different things all rolled into one. It means:

I feel frustrated.

I feel anxious.

I feel overwhelmed.

I feel freaked out.

😞 I feel unhappy.

😖 I feel defeated.

😣 I feel stressed.

😵 I feel powerless and like I don't have control over my own life!

Anyone who says this phrase can mean any or all of these things. But this last sentence, I find, seems to apply especially to teens.

Why? Because when you're a teenager, that phrase can often feel, well, true. (Just because it *feels* true doesn't mean it is true, but more on that in a bit.)

"BUT THESE ARE THE BEST YEARS OF YOUR LIFE!"

Have you ever expressed unhappiness about some part of your life to a random adult—maybe a parent or a grandparent or your friend's parent or a teacher at school—only to have the grown-up get a sort of wistful, googly-eyed look on his or her face and respond with some version of the phrase "But these are the best years of your life!"? Well, if you ask me, that person probably doesn't have a very good memory of what being a teenager is actually like. Or that person is remembering only the good parts and forgetting about the bad. (Then again, maybe it's harder to be a teen these days than it was when he or she was growing up.)

But I remember a lot of it, which is one of the main reasons I wanted to write this book. I remember what it was like to be a teenager growing up in a small town near Melbourne, Australia, born smack-dab in the middle of seven children. With three brothers and three sisters. I loved my family (and still do), but I remember often feeling frustrated because I had the distinct feeling that I wasn't in control of my own life. That I was expected to behave a certain way, to think certain things, to want certain things. And that these expectations weren't always in line with what I actually believed or what I actually wanted.

THE CLUTTER OF TOO MANY HAVE-TOS

Being a teenager is hard, for a whole lot of reasons, not least of which is the fact that you are living in someone else's house. And that means you end up having to, for the most part, do what they say. (The perennial parental favorite, "While you live under my roof, you'll live by my rules!" is a favorite for a reason.)

Your life is full of too many *have-los*. You have to wake up early, and you have to go to school; you have to spend all day going to a whole bunch of different classes, most of which you probably

didn't get to pick. After school you might have to go to a sports practice or a meeting for a club or a rehearsal for a play. Or maybe you have to go to an after-school job. After that you have to come home, and you have to do homework. Then you have to help out around the house. Maybe you have to look after a little brother or sister. And it probably doesn't end

there. It can often feel like a lot—like *all*—of your time is spent doing things that other people tell you to do. That your day is not your own. That you are powerless and don't have any control over your own life. But what I hope you might get from this book is the feeling, and the knowledge, that a lot more parts of your life are within your control than you might think.

And no, I'm not going to tell you that you don't actually have to go to school. And that you can blow off all your chores and forget about your homework. And that your five-year-old brother can just take care of himself. Don't try to get me in trouble, now!

What I'm saying is this:

YOU can
DO ANYTHING
YOU
SET YOUR MIND TO

"You can do anything you set your mind to" is probably a phrase you've heard before. Maybe you've heard it from *many* well-meaning adults. It's one of those phrases people love to toss around. Maybe you've heard it so much that you're sick of hearing it, or maybe you've heard it so much that as soon as you hear it (or read it), you tune it out. And you

have forgotten that it means anything at all. What it means is this: You don't have to simply go through life waiting for your life to happen *to* you. You can make things happen. Things can change. You can change. And no matter how overwhelming your clutter situation might be right now, *that can change too.*

But when you're thinking about your goals, make sure they're *your* goals. Not society's goals, not your parents' goals, not your friends' goals. *Your* goals.

If you're five feet tall and the last time you dunked a basketball was when you were four (and it was one of those little Nerf basketballs and you walked right up to the hoop and put the ball directly in it), chances are you are not going to join the NBA. And if you can barely sing a note, and dogs start howling every time you try to, it's rather unlikely that you will be a professional opera singer. And if you put your mind to it, even if you *really, really, really* put your mind to it, you're probably not going to wake up one morning having sprouted wings with which you can fly around your room.

BUT if you put your mind to it, you can certainly get creative and, say, start a basketball league for the less tall, less hoops-shootingly gifted. Or produce a special silent opera where you open your mouth but don't sing out loud, or one where the audience listens to

an iPod of someone else singing while you pretend to. And hey, if you end up inventing a pair of electric wings a person can use to fly around the house, well, I'd like to buy the first pair, please.

However, please keep in mind— just because you might want to *put your mind to* packing every item of clothing you have ever owned since you were six years old into your dresser doesn't mean it's going to happen. And just because you might want to *put your mind to* keeping every issue of every magazine that has ever entered your house on one shelf of your bookcase does not mean they will fit. *Putting your mind to* things cannot change the laws of physics, or the laws of time and space, or the laws of thermodynamics, or the laws of probability.

Your mind is a powerful thing! But you have to know what you're up against.

So, back to my point: The phrase "You can do anything you put your mind to" means that you can and should have goals. And that you can and should believe in yourself. But when you set your mind to something, make sure it's your *own* goal, one that will serve the future you are trying to create. The future is wide open to you. And that is a very exciting thing! (*But it can also be a scary thing too.*)

NOT JUST THE FUTURE, BUT NOW!

But wait, what about now? Isn't *now* important too? Well, yes, in fact it is. It is quite important, actually. You, right now, sitting there reading this, have the power to not only change your situation in the future, but to change your situation starting at this very moment. The life you're trying to create is not just a life you'll be living in the future, but one you are living *right now.*

I know, I know—it sounds like a bunch of self-help-booky, grown-ups-saying-stuff-that-they-think-is-nice-to-say-to-teens-but-that-no-one-really-believes crap. Hearing "inspiring" stuff without hearing any information to back it up can make a person, well, stop listening after a while.

What if it's not just a bunch of crap? Just for the length of time it takes you to read this book, I'm asking you to keep an open mind and accept the possibility that maybe, just maybe, things can change. And maybe this book can help.

"But wait!" you might be saying. "Isn't this a book on *decluttering*? And isn't 'decluttering' a fancy word for just cleaning your room? Because having a clean room is nice and all, but I really don't see how that's going to *change my life*."

Okay, I hear you. But the answers to your questions are: yes (among other things) and no! Just go with me here. Before we get into the nitty-gritty of decluttering, before we talk about your relationship with *stuff* and how it's affecting you, think about this question:

WHAT DO YOU WANT FROM YOUR LIFE RIGHT NOW?

Not what you want ten years from now, five years from now, or a year from now, but your vision for your own life today. *Today.* Weird as it might sound, this is *the* most important question to ask yourself in the decluttering process. Think about it just for a moment now, and we will discuss it again later.

When you're a teenager, there's a lot of emphasis on your future. Where are you going to college? What do you want to be when you grow up? I'm not trying to say you don't need to think about it at all; surely, some planning is important, and you need to do it. But with all the emphasis put on the future, it's easy to forget that you're alive *right now* and that what is going on now matters too. In fact it matters a whole lot.

And one of the main things that take people out of the moment they're in and make them miss it entirely is clutter. Mental clutter, emotional clutter, internal clutter, and physical clutter. The clutter of our expectations. Clutter robs us of the best parts of life and keeps us from enjoying *now.* And the thing is, it's *always* now. It will always be now. It will never not be now. (I once saw a watch on which the face always said, simply, NOW. Not super convenient when one has to be at a particular place at a particular hour. But, still, that watch had a good point!)

THIS IS YOUR LIFE. YOU'RE LIVING IT!

I remember being a teen and having the feeling that I was waiting for my actual life to start. Like the life I was living then was just preparation, was just the preview to the main show. I just had this feeling that as soon as I became a grown-up my Real Life would begin. But you know what? I look back on those times and I realize that during those years, while I was spending so much time worrying about the future, I was missing out on the present.

We *do* need to plan for the future—don't get me wrong. All of us do. The future is coming whether we like it or not, and it always helps to have some sort of a plan for it. However, there is a difference between preparing for the future and spending all our time worrying about it and obsessing about it. Worrying and obsessing do not help you meet your goals. Worrying and obsessing do not help you get the life you want. (Unless what you want is a life full of worry and obsession, that is. And I am guessing you do not!)

When I was a teenager spending all my time planning for what was to come, my real life was *already* going on. And so is yours. *This is your life, right now. You are living it.*

But are you having as much fun as you could be? Are you are happy as you could be? Are you enjoying life as much as you could be? Or are you being robbed by clutter?

CHAPTER SUMMARY . . .

In this chapter we talked about your goals, your life, thinking toward the future, and living in the now. We talked about the clutter of too many have-tos and how being a teen can be fun and exciting, but it can also be really stressful. We also introduced the most important question when it comes to decluttering: *What do you want from your life right now?*

WHAT COMES NEXT . . .

There are lots of different kinds of clutter. In the next chapter we'll talk about some of the different kinds of internal clutter that affect teens the most. The Internal Clutter Quiz will help you identify what's affecting you!

No matter what Devon DiSapoint does, it never seems to be enough. At least so far as his parents are concerned. He knows they love him, and he knows that they only expect so much from him because they believe he is capable of a lot. But sometimes it seems to Devon like their expectations are just too high! For example: Last week Devon took a science test. He got a 92, which he thought was a pretty good score. But his mom was so upset that he hadn't gotten a 100 that she just let out one of those big sighs that make Devon cringe. "How are you going to get into a good college with an average score like that?" she said. And his dad just nodded in agreement.

Devon wanted to point out that a 92 is *not* an average score; it is actually a very good score. But there was just no reasoning with them, so he didn't even try. Suddenly his 92 did not seem like such a good grade after all, and he felt disappointed. Disappointed that *they* were disappointed. And also disappointed in himself.

This is not the first time he's felt like that. Pretty much every time he takes a test at school or writes a paper, his parents are upset if he gets anything less than a 100 or an A-plus. And if he does get a 100 or an A-plus, they want to know why he didn't get extra credit. And if he gets extra credit . . . somehow they still don't seem happy!

And it doesn't stop there. When he was elected vice president of the debate club, they were upset that he wasn't president. When he was put in two advanced classes, they wanted to know why it wasn't three. And no matter how many times he tried to explain that he couldn't be cocaptain of the track team *and* captain of the swim team because both teams practice at the same time, his parents just didn't quite get it.

Their expectations feel like a giant mountain that he has to climb, but no matter how fast he climbs and how high he climbs, no matter how hard he pushes himself, the top just keeps getting farther and farther away. And he is completely out of breath!

CHAPTER 2

INTERNAL CLUTTER

Internal clutter can be some of the trickiest kind of clutter to see. Why? Well, because it's all inside you. It can be inside your brain, covered with your skull and your skin and your hair. Maybe even a hat! Internal clutter can also live inside your stomach, where it makes you feel sick. Or throughout your entire body, where it makes you feel achy and stressed. And what's a big source of clutter in most teens' lives? The clutter of expectations.

If you're cluttered with too many expectations coming from too many different sources, chances are you're going to feel unhappy, anxious, stressed, and even depressed. Three of the most common sources of teen internal clutter are the clutter of your parents' expectations, the clutter of your friends' expectations, and the clutter of your own expectations.

Don't get me wrong—I'm not saying no one should ever expect anything from you. In fact it can be nice when people expect things of you. When you know people in your life believe in you enough to expect you to do fantastic things, well, that's just great. What's not nice is when the expectations seem unrealistic, and instead of filling you with pride, they fill you with anxiety and dread. And when other people's (or your own) expectations fill you with anxiety and dread, this is how you know they've become clutter.

And clutter of *any kind* is stressful to deal with.

Although internal clutter and external clutter might *seem* like two different things, here's the funny part: Often, *internal clutter manifests itself as external clutter.* Which is to say that when we feel cluttered on the inside, we often make clutter on the outside. When we feel anxious or depressed or out of control, when we feel burdened by the weight of the world, our surroundings become more chaotic. External clutter might *seem* like

WHEN WE FEEL CLUTTERED ON THE INSIDE, WE OFTEN MAKE CLUTTER ON THE OUTSIDE.

the problem, since it's easier to spot than internal clutter, but the truth is, you pretty much never get one without the other.

So when you want to start thinking about how to get rid of external clutter for good, the first step isn't to think about throwing stuff away—it's to think about your *internal clutter*. And the biggest and most important step in clearing your internal clutter is understanding where it comes from.

Oftentimes our minds are so full of internal clutter coming from so many sources that we can't even begin to identify the clutter for what it is. We just know we feel anxious, stressed, or depressed and don't know why! Only when we understand it can we begin to let it go—to clear the clutter from our minds and from our lives. The Internal Clutter Quiz on the next page will help you figure out the source of some of your internal clutter.

INTERNAL CLUTTER

WHERE DOES MOST OF YOURS COME FROM?

I You get your science midterm back and even though you studied, it turns out you got a D-minus. What's your first thought?

A *My parents are going to be so upset, and I feel awful for letting them down. I can already imagine what my dad's face will look like when he sees it. He'll give me that look, the one where he wrinkles his forehead and it looks like two caterpillars are crawling toward each other. Two sad caterpillars walking toward each other to cry because of how disappointed they are. And he is!*

B *Dude, I'm just glad the teacher passed back the tests facedown. If any of my friends saw this, I'd be really embarrassed.*

C *I am going to barf over how disappointed I am. I studied, and I thought I knew the material. Maybe twenty hours of studying wasn't enough. Maybe I should do thirty next time. Or forty! Argh. How could I let this happen?*

2 You've just realized that you signed up for too many extracurricular activities and you're not going to have time for all of them. You're thinking of dropping yearbook, but the idea fills you with anxiety. Why?

A *My parents expect me to be able to handle everything. I wouldn't want to let them down!*

B *Some of my friends are on yearbook. If I drop out now, they'll have more work to do. And that's not fair to them.*

C *Because I shouldn't have to drop something. I should be able to get it all done.*

3 It's time for the prom. You're not necessarily so jazzed about the idea, but you wouldn't dare skip it because:

A *Your parents had a great time at their proms and you know they'd be really sad if you missed yours. Your mom has been waiting for this day since you were a little kid!*

B *Your friends are all going, and you know they would be bummed if you weren't there.*

C *Even though you don't necessarily want to go, you feel like you should go. I mean, isn't going to prom just what people do?*

4 You met a cute guy/girl in your English class. The two of you studied together a few times and clearly you liked each other. After a while you started making plans to hang out. And the more you hung out, the more you wanted to hang out. Now things are starting to get more serious. What are you most likely to worry about?

A *I hope my parents like him/her. It's not that I'm worried they'll say I'm not allowed to date him/her, it's just that their opinion is the most important thing to me. I could never go out with someone they didn't like.*

B *I hope my friends like him/her. He/she is a little bit geeky, and I don't want them to make fun of me for it.*

C *I hope I don't screw anything up. If I say even one dumb thing or make even one wrong move, I am going to obsess about it forever and never let myself forget it! This relationship will only work if I am completely perfect and never make any mistakes.*

5

You've been super busy lately, what with school, extracurriculars, studying, doing chores around the house, and your part-time job. Now it's your first free Saturday afternoon in a month. You love your family and friends, but you really need to have some time alone to just relax—maybe read a book, or watch your favorite TV show, or surf the Internet, or just hang out with your thoughts. What's most likely to pull you away from that?

A *My parents. I know they keep saying I'm not spending enough time with the family lately. If I have a free afternoon, they'll probably expect me to spend it helping with more chores around the house.*

B *I know my friends have been a little annoyed at how I've kind of vanished lately. If they find out that I have a free afternoon, it'll really hurt their feelings if I don't go hang out with them wherever they are.*

C *I'll feel like I'm wasting time if I just relax and do nothing. More than likely I'll end up doing something productive like working on my college applications or trying to get a head start on some school projects. I can rest after high school is over. Or maybe when college is over. Or . . . y'know, later.*

Now tally up how many *A*s, *B*s, and *C*s you have, and consult the key below.

NOTE

You can be affected by more than one kind of internal clutter. In fact most people are.

IF YOU CHOSE MOSTLY *A*s: You're cluttered with . . . *the clutter of parental expectations.* Pretty much all teens have some parental expectation clutter. And really, when it's in moderation, you don't even need to call it clutter. Because some amount is normal and healthy and can benefit your life. There is nothing wrong with wanting to make your parents proud and letting their belief in you spur you toward meeting some of your goals. But parental expectations become a problem when they govern your entire life and you are unable to distinguish what you want from your life and what *they* want from your life. As your parents it's their job to try to help you do your best. However, as a person who is well on your way to becoming an adult, it's your job to make sure that you're doing what makes *you* happy, not just what someone else thinks will make you happy. I'm not saying you shouldn't listen to your parents. I'm just saying that if you find you're spending most of your time and energy worrying about making sure your parents are happy, it might be time to step back and think about what *you* want. They are your parents, and it's their job to help you do your best, but your life is your life. So make sure you're okay with the life you've created, because you're the only one who has to live it.

IF YOU CHOSE MOSTLY *B*s: You're cluttered with . . . *the clutter of your friends' expectations.* It can be a great thing when friends inspire each other to push themselves and reach their goals. In fact friends *should* help each other to do their best. But sometimes we care so much what our friends think and we get so consumed with pleasing our friends that we confuse their thoughts with our thoughts and their goals with our goals. And that's when it becomes a problem. We should be around people who inspire us, but we should also understand that the life we want for ourselves and the one they want for themselves might not be the same thing.

IF YOU CHOSE MOSTLY *C*s: You're cluttered with . . . *the clutter of your own expectations.* You know that you're capable of doing fantastic things, so you expect a lot from yourself. Good for you! But there's a big difference between wanting to do your best and expecting to be *perfect*. You are human, and like every other human on this planet you will make mistakes. So when you're thinking about what you expect from yourself, make sure it's reasonable. And make sure that your ambitions serve to make your life more exciting and interesting, not just more filled with anxiety.

ANOTHER KIND OF INTERNAL CLUTTER

We all suffer from it (it's almost impossible not to): *the clutter of society's expectations.* Being part of a community, being part of a society, means—at least in part—being influenced by what society believes we should have, do, and be. To some extent our goals for ourselves *always* come from the society in which we live. Think about the most basic things you are planning for your future: For most teens this includes graduating high school, going to college, and getting a job of some kind. If you lived a thousand, five hundred, or even just a hundred years ago, what you wanted and expected out of life would not be what you want and expect now. Having the goals of a person who lived five thousand years ago wouldn't make sense today. We're all influenced by the society in which we live.

However, being influenced by society's expectations becomes a problem when our views of what we "should" be and what we "should" want are influenced by sometimes unhelpful and potentially misleading sources. TV shows, movies, magazines, the Internet—these can all be great sources of entertainment, and even education. But the latest episode of *Gossip Girl* or issue of *Us Weekly* might not be the best place to get ideas for reasonable goals for your own life. Anyone who consumes any type of mass media (i.e., almost everyone) is inundated with images of "perfect" people living "perfect" lives. And seeing all these "perfect" people and their "perfect" lives, our brains end up cluttered with ideas of what we're being told we "should" want, which may or may not bear any resemblance to what we actually want, or what would make us happy deep down. But simply being aware that this may be happening can do a lot toward waking us up and making sure that our own goals are actually ours.

SOME MORE QUESTIONS TO CONSIDER WHEN THINKING ABOUT YOUR INTERNAL CLUTTER

- Do I spend a lot of time worrying about what will happen to me in the future?

- Do I think that worrying about the future will help me prevent bad things from happening?

- Do I spend a lot of time fantasizing about the future and how things will be different for me then?

- Do I keep myself away from the present moment by constantly being "somewhere else" inside my head?

- Do I spend a lot of time reminiscing about the past or thinking about some imagined better time in my life?

- Do I spend a lot of time missing "the way things were"?

- Do I spend a lot of time regretting things I've done in the past?

In asking you to consider these questions, I don't mean to imply that thinking about the past or planning for what's to come is always a bad thing. Some amount of reflection and planning is necessary and required for a happy and healthy life. It's when your main focus becomes things that may or may not happen, or things that are already over and done with, that you run into problems.

As I mentioned before, internal and external clutter are closely related. One affects the other, and both keep you from enjoying the present. So now it's time to look *outside* at the junk that is clogging up your room, your locker, your backpack, and your car. The stuff that probably inspired you (or someone who cares about you) to get this book in the first place. So let's start taking stock!

CHAPTER SUMMARY . . .

Other people's (and your own) expectations can add to your life, but they can also be a huge source of clutter. When you're thinking about what you want for yourself and your life, it's important to make sure your goals are *your goals* and not someone else's.

WHAT COMES NEXT . . .

In the next chapter we'll begin to look at your *external* clutter. What is it? How did it get there? How is it affecting your life?

Ever since sixth grade Jasmine and her two best friends have spent pretty much all their free time shopping. And now, three years later, it's still true. The mall is pretty much the only place Jasmine can go with her friends where they're guaranteed privacy, with no little brothers eavesdropping and no little sisters trying to tag along. Better yet, there are no parents there telling them to do their homework and to turn down the music.

The mall is like their clubhouse. They like to walk around and see who else they know is there. And they like to look for cute guys from other schools and flirt with them in front of the Cinnabon.

Oh, and of course they like to buy stuff.

Shopping is one of Jasmine's favorite pastimes. When she's shopping, she really feels like she's *doing something* that might improve her life and help her figure out who she is. Jasmine is smack in the middle of five kids, you see. Her older sister is really into sports—she's on two varsity teams and is even training for a marathon. Her older brother is really into writing—he writes poems and short stories, and he's editor of their school's literary magazine. Her younger brother is a fantastic singer and always gets all the solos in chorus. Her younger sister is an amazing artist—she's already sold one of her paintings, and she's only ten!

But Jasmine doesn't know *what* she likes to do! What's her "thing"? Where does she fit in?

She has no idea, but every time she walks into her local mall, she feels certain that just waiting inside one of those hundred fifty-six stores is something, some special item or outfit or gadget or lotion or hair product or piece of equipment, that will help her figure out who she is and what she's really good at.

Well, so far she knows one thing she's really good at: turning her babysitting money and birthday money into piles and piles of useless stuff. Now her room is packed with random things she never uses—castoffs from hobbies she's tried and rejected. If you go into her room, you'll find balls of yarn and knitting needles and crochet hooks from the time she thought she might start making her own sweaters. You'll find a bunch of pieces of felt and some ribbons from the time she was thinking of making a bunch of felt wallets and selling them online. You'll find a set of five different harmonicas and a bunch of sheet music and some CDs on harmonica instruction. You'll find a stack of fifteen out-of-date magazines—everything from *Cat Fancy* and *Knitting Quarterly* to *Gardening Times* and *Everything Scrapbooking*. And that's just on the nightstand next to her bed!

Last week Jasmine and her two best friends went to the mall. After walking around for a little while, they went over to one of their favorite trendy discount stores. They all decided to try on the same dress, just for fun, in different colors. It looked really cute on her two best friends, but it didn't really suit Jasmine that well. It was too long and tight in some areas and loose in others, and okay, let's just be honest here . . . it made her look like a potato. But her two best friends were both going to buy it, and they wanted her to buy it too. And the last thing she wanted was to be left out! Besides, she thought, maybe the dress would look good when she was a little older. A little taller, maybe. So she bought it anyway; after all, it *was* 50 percent off.

When she got home, do you know what she did with her new dress? She shoved it directly into the back of her closet. There was nowhere else for it to fit!

Every time Jasmine looks at her piles of stuff, she feels, well . . . not the way she was hoping she would when she bought it. She thought the stuff would make her feel confident in herself and excited for life. Creative and inspired. Instead she feels anxious, stressed, ashamed, and just overall BAD! Bad about all the projects she's started and never finished, bad because of all the money she's wasted, bad because she still doesn't know who she wants to be and what she wants to do. And, most importantly, bad because her room is *so cluttered* she can barely think! She wishes she just had a big plastic box she could shove everything in so she could forget about it. Only problem is, it'd have to be a *magic box* that shrank everything you put inside it; otherwise it'd be too big to fit through the door!

CHAPTER 3

EXTERNAL CLUTTER
(a.K.a. STUFF!)

No matter your personality,
no matter your personal style, no matter how you
think and how you like to do things, the stuff you
surround yourself with affects how you feel. This
is a simple fact. All humans are affected by our
environments. It's impossible for us not to be!

But sometimes we're affected more than we even
realized. If you spend a lot of time in a messy,
cluttered room, eventually your brain might begin to
block out your conscious awareness of the clutter.
(It's like how most people don't register the smell of
their own shampoo.) You might not wake up every

morning in the clutter and think, "Oh, no! It's the clutter!" But trust me, the unconscious part of your brain still knows what you're dealing with!

Instead of consciously having *thoughts* about it, you'll just have feelings about it. Feelings of anxiety, depression, and powerlessness. And you might not even know where those feelings came from! I don't mean to imply that *all* of the problems in your life come from having too much stuff. Life is more complex than that. But what I *am* saying is that having too much stuff surely isn't helping! It's impossible to work on *anything* in your life when you're drowning in clutter.

Stuff steals time. Stuff steals money. Stuff steals life! When you're inundated with clutter, so much of your brainpower is being used just dealing with it that it's hard to think about anything else.

Imagine trying to reflect on an important decision in the middle of a busy city street surrounded by lights and noise with cars coming toward you in both directions. It'd be hard to concentrate, wouldn't it? Well, a cluttered room is like that busy street.

AREN'T CONVINCED THAT YOUR SURROUNDINGS AFFECT HOW YOU FEEL?

HERE'S AN EXERCISE YOU CAN TRY RIGHT NOW.

Imagine your favorite place, or even just a place you really like. This can either be a place you've been before or one you've just made up in your head. A beach, perhaps, or a waterfall in the mountains. Close your eyes and really think about it for two full minutes. What does this place smell like? What does this place sound like? What does this place look like? Imagine the colors you'd see and the textures you'd touch. When two minutes are up, open your eyes. Do you feel different? A little calmer, maybe? A little more relaxed?

You probably do. And that's just from *two minutes* of *thinking* about a place. Imagine how different it would be if you were actually there!

But just as positive, relaxing places can affect us positively, negative spaces can affect us negatively. I won't ask you to imagine yourself living in a garbage dump, or a damp basement . . . but you get the idea.

STUFF as a manifestation of internal clutter

Your surroundings affect how you feel, but the flip side is also true—how you feel affects your surroundings. People make the spaces they inhabit match their mood, even without thinking about it.

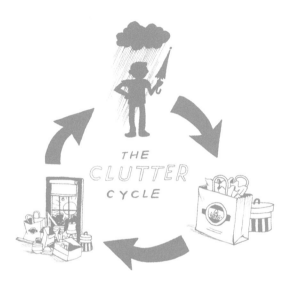

THE CLUTTER CYCLE

That's the funny, confusing thing about clutter—it can be both the cause and the effect. When you are cluttered internally, you make clutter in your surroundings. And when your surroundings are cluttered, you will feel more cluttered inside. Clutter feeds off itself. Clutter blocks all the light out of a room (both literally and figuratively). Clutter blocks the energy in a room and exhausts the people in it. Put a calm, organized, happy person in a very cluttered space, hide all the stuff they need under piles and piles of useless other stuff, and after not too long they'll find themselves feeling more frustrated, anxious, and unhappy. And overall more cluttery!

And put an anxious, depressed, cluttered person in a serene and neat space, and after not too long they'll find themselves cluttering it up. That's why you can't simply clean your room, toss out all your clutter, and expect your life to change completely. You'll just end up going right back to the way things were! The only way to get out of the clutter cycle is to break it.

But it's a hard cycle to break! Especially when so many of our recreational activities and social interactions revolve around Getting New Stuff.

THE LURE OF THE MALL

While most people's mall addiction might not be as severe as Jasmine Jumbleton's, the truth is that we are a country full of people obsessed with malls. We use malls as places to shop, to socialize, to grab a snack, to skateboard, to relax. We go to the mall to see movies and to get haircuts. The Mall of America even has an amusement park right inside!

But malls don't just promise us goods and services (and an occasional ride on a giant roller coaster); they promise (often falsely) to sell us items that will *help us define who we are.*

Most people enter the mall in one of two mind-sets. In the first, we go to the mall with an idea in mind of some particular item or type of item we want or need. (Perhaps an outfit for a relative's wedding or a dance at school, or a gift for someone's birthday.) More likely, we go to the mall in the second mind-set—with the vague idea that we *might* need something (although we're not entirely sure what this is), and we decide we'll browse at our favorite go-to stores until something calls out to us promising to improve our lives. The problem is that nine times out of ten we're *not* actually buying things that will improve our lives. Most of the time what we end up coming home with are impulse buys—things we neither want nor need, things that we only bought because we were intoxicated by the store's fluorescent lighting, chirpy salespeople, and peppy dance music. And once we get them home, these things end up adding to our mass of clutter and making our lives worse.

HERE'S a LIST of some of the items you might find yourself coming home with after a visit to the mall, even when you weren't looking for anything in particular. Think back to everything you've bought in the last month. Put one check mark for each item you've bought in each of the following categories.

- PERSONAL CARE PRODUCTS (including but not limited to cologne/perfume, body spray, bath gel, lotion, face products, hair products, nail polish)

- CLOTHES (I won't explain this, because I think you know what clothes are.)

- BOOKS (You probably know what books are too.)

- GAMES (video games, card games, equipment for online games)

- SPORTS/FITNESS EQUIPMENT (workout DVDs, yoga mats, specialty sports apparel)

- ART/CRAFT SUPPLIES (paint, clay, drawing pencils, ink, paper, canvas, wire, pliers, yarn, knitting needles)

- ENTERTAINMENT (DVDs, CDs, iPod, iPod accessories, video games)

Now, tally up the number of items you've bought in each of these categories. And begin to ask yourself what feeling you were trying to buy when you bought the items you did. Keep this list handy when we move on to the next chapter.

What counts as external clutter?

If I'm going to keep on about all this "clutter," it'd probably be a good idea to give a list of some of the items I'm talking about. Have you ever heard the old saying that goes "One man's trash is another one's treasure"? Well, going along with that, one man's (or woman's) treasure is another one's clutter! Just because an item is "valuable" or "useful" does not mean it is not cluttering up your life. Please remember that this is only a partial list to help you get started.

I'D CALL THIS CLUTTER:

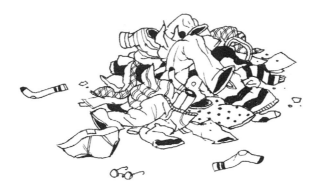

- **ANY EVERYDAY CLOTHING ITEMS** that you have not worn in the past six months.

- **ANY CLOTHING ITEMS THAT DON'T FLATTER YOU OR FIT YOU** *at this exact moment.*

- **ANY "SPECIAL OCCASION" CLOTHING ITEMS** that you have not worn in the last year.

- **COPIES OF USEFUL ITEMS THAT YOU ALREADY OWN** and use regularly but can only use one of. (This is a super popular type of clutter, especially when it comes to teens. For example, you probably don't need two iPods, two cell phones, two alarm clocks, or two calendars.)

- **ANYTHING EXPIRED OR OUT OF DATE.**

- **ANY PERSONAL CARE PRODUCTS YOU DON'T USE** (perfumes and colognes you no longer wear, makeup that doesn't look good on you after all, lotion that makes you break out or makes you itchy, shampoo that smells weird, conditioner that makes your hair greasy, deodorant that smells like old people—you get the picture).

- **TRASH.** (This should be obvious, but it is still worth mentioning—random scraps of paper, old napkins, coffee cups, plastic water bottles.)

- **RANDOM PROMOTIONAL ITEMS THAT YOU DON'T USE DAILY.** (This might include free T-shirts, pens, Frisbees, key chains, stress balls, magnets, clips, sticky pads, highlighters, and anything else that was given to you free for promotional purposes.)

- **BOOKS YOU'VE READ OR OUTGROWN** and will not likely read again.

- **NOTEBOOKS** from years past.

- **BINDERS** from years past.

- **OLD CLASS NOTES** that you've since recopied or typed into your computer.

- **EXTRA BLANKETS** that you never use.

- **SHEETS AND PILLOWCASES** that you never use.

- **EXTRA HANGERS** in your closet.

- **DEAD PLANTS.**

- **SINGLE SOCKS.**

- **SINGLE EARRINGS.**

- **ITEMS THAT YOU CAN'T USE** until you fix them,

which have been sitting in your room broken for more than a month.

- GIFTS YOU DO NOT USE.

- ITEMS THAT BELONG TO OTHER PEOPLE.

- THINGS YOU'RE SAVING for a future that might not happen.

- SPORTS EQUIPMENT for sports you no longer play.

- HOBBY SUPPLIES for hobbies you're no longer into.

"Neat" CLUTTER IS STILL CLUTTER

It's easy to spot clutter when it's in a big messy pile on your floor. But what about when your clutter is "organized"? What about when you're keeping your clutter carefully hidden inside a dresser or at the back of a closet or inside a nice set of pretty boxes or colorful containers? What if your clutter is all stacked in very neat stacks all around your room? It might seem like this clutter doesn't "count" somehow, but I assure you, it does! Organized clutter is every bit as destructive and life-sucking as messy clutter, and even potentially more so, because it's easier to kid yourself that it's okay to keep it! Simply making your clutter look presentable is not the same thing as getting rid of it.

ALL STUFF ISN'T BaD

Make no mistake—I'm not trying to say that all stuff is bad. While there is very little a person actually "needs" to survive, I'll be the first to admit that there is plenty of stuff that can improve your life. Having a nice framed photograph of your friends in a cool frame on your wall can make you happy whenever you look at it. Having a really fantastic and flattering outfit can make you feel great every time you put it on. It's nice to have an interesting book to read and a fun and entertaining game to play. A cozy bed to sleep in and a nice room to wake up to can be a great source of joy. But we are all conditioned to be so into our stuff that it is easy to assume that the fix for any bad feeling or problem we're having lies at the nearest department store. And while buying stuff can temporarily distract us from whatever is wrong, the solution to any problem seldom lies in cluttering our bedrooms, closets, backpacks, and cars with useless stuff. So when it comes to stuff, where do we draw the line? How much is too much? And how do we go about figuring this out?

Internal clutter and external clutter are intrinsically linked. If you're internally cluttered, you'll make external clutter. And if you're externally cluttered, you'll feel cluttered inside! Your surroundings affect how you feel, maybe more than you even notice. While all "stuff" isn't bad, even useful, "valuable" items can become clutter if they're not serving your goals and your life.

WHAT COMES NEXT . . .

In the next chapter we'll talk about how imagining the life you want to live is *the* most important thing to do when it comes to getting clutter-free.

Sheila McShambles has tried getting organized before.
She's tried lots of times, in fact! Every six months or
so she'll look around her room (which is usually in
shambles) and she'll decide it's time to reign in the clutter
and get organized. Once and for all!

She'll be filled with tons of energy and inspiration at
first. So she'll get up early on a Saturday morning and

convince her older brother to drive her to the local organizing store (even though he *really* doesn't like getting up early, and she usually has to bribe him by offering to do all his chores for a couple of weeks). Once there she'll buy lots of helpful organizational tools, like nice big storage boxes covered in pretty patterned paper and big under-bed boxes with plastic tops. These boxes will probably end up costing quite a lot, but she'll convince herself it's worth it, because these boxes are going to help her start her brand-new, neater, more organized life.

When she gets home, she'll spend the next couple of hours taking all the stuff that's cluttering her desk and bed and floor and packing it up in her brand-new pretty boxes. She won't get rid of anything, mind you, but she'll make it look pretty—temporarily. As she closes the lid of the last box, she'll think, *Problem solved!* And she'll feel really good.

The only thing is, the problem is never "solved" for very long.

For a couple of weeks Sheila will be super diligent about trying to keep her room clean and her stuff in order. She'll put all her clothes directly in the laundry hamper when she's done wearing them, and she'll make sure not to leave extra water glasses on her nightstand. For those first couple of weeks after a big cleaning, she'll have this funny feeling, every time she walks into her room, that she may in fact have stepped into someone else's room.

But then, inevitably, the mess will begin to creep out of the boxes and back into her living space. After all, she hasn't gotten rid of anything; she's just hidden it away.

Maybe one day she'll be late for school and will decide at the last second to change outfits, so she'll leave a pair of jeans and a few tops tossed onto her desk chair. Or maybe she'll eat a bowl of cereal right before bed and leave the bowl and spoon on top of her dresser. Or maybe she'll be wrapping a present for a birthday party and will leave the wrapping paper and scissors and tape on her floor. Or maybe she'll just realize that she's packed away something she really likes/wants/needs, and she'll have to toss everything out of all her boxes in order to find it.

Well, *however* the first few pieces of clutter escape from their boxes, it seems like once one little piece of mess works its way out, the rest gets jealous and follows it. Within a month of Sheila's decluttering, her room is back to normal, except that it's more cluttered now because she has all those fancy, "helpful" boxes taking up even more space. It's very disheartening! She'll be so discouraged that she'll just live in the mess for another few months before she'll try again. And again. And again.

But Sheila just doesn't understand why! After all, she makes the effort—she spends the money on the boxes and puts things in them. So why doesn't that seem to be enough? *What* is she missing? How can she get off this clutter roller coaster once and for all?

CHAPTER 4

THE MOST IMPORTANT QUESTION

WHEN IT COMES TO YOUR CLUTTER

Before we continue, let's just
get one thing straight—the reason to declutter
yourself/your room/your life is not because clean is
holy and messy is evil. It's not because clean people
are good and messy people are bad. Perhaps this
seems like an obvious point, but it's worth mentioning,
because despite how silly it is, I think a lot of people
actually believe it. But the truth is this: *The state of
your room is not a moral issue.* And neither is the state
of your locker, your backpack, or the trunk of your car.

The reason to purge your clutter and organize your
life is not because it will make you a holier person

somehow. It's not so you can brag to people that you are neat and clean while they are messy and gross. It's not to make society happy. It's not to make your parents happy or to make your siblings happy (although this may be a great side effect). The reason to purge your clutter, to get yourself organized, and to change your relationship with *stuff* is because *it will improve your life.* And not just in the obvious ways, but in all sorts of ways that may not, at first, even seem connected to the clutter.

Any goal you have for yourself, whether it's getting a spot on the varsity soccer team or getting the lead in the school play or being made editor of the yearbook, will be easier to reach if you are not overrun with clutter—if you don't have clutter holding you back. (Well, unless your goal is to win the Most Cluttered Person in the World contest, and then I suppose being really cluttered would be a plus.) That is not just my opinion as a professional organizer. That is my belief as a person who has seen this happen hundreds of times. When very cluttered people get rid of their extra stuff and change their relationship with their stuff, it is actually quite common that they suddenly find themselves better able to reach their goals in other seemingly unrelated areas of their lives.

SO HOW DO I GET STARTED?

What I'm about to say might surprise you—in
fact at first it might sound downright wacky—but
get ready; here it goes: *When it comes to getting
organized, it's not really about the stuff.* I know,
that sounds crazy, especially coming from a
professional organizer and the guy who's been
talking about "stuff" for the last seventy-four
pages. But the truth is, getting your life in order
isn't just a matter of getting organized. Not really.

When people first decide to get their lives in order,
they usually think in terms of boxes and bags. In
terms of storage trunks and new shelves. But when
you're getting ready to change your clutter situation,
the most important question you can ask yourself
has nothing to do with how many big plastic boxes to
buy or what color photo boxes to use. It has nothing
to do with whether you should buy a filing cabinet or
a magazine rack. It has nothing to do with how you
should organize your DVD collection. All that stuff
comes *later.*

If you're looking to make real changes in your life,
in your surroundings, the most important thing to do
before you even begin is this: *Imagine the life you
want to live.*

This is *the* most important thing to think about when it comes to decluttering, or organizing, or making any big changes in your life, really. I'll say it again:

Imagine the life you want to live.

Now ask yourself: How can I achieve the life I want to live?

That's it. It's that simple.

Only it's really not simple at all. As important as this question is, as *life-changing* as this question is, it's one that a lot of people never even think to ask themselves. Yet it can play a vital role in reshaping every area of our lives, from our rooms and our backpacks to our relationships with our friends and family.

You might wonder: If this is such an important question, why don't people bring it up more often?

Probably because it forces us to face our situation head-on, and that invites change into our lives. And let's be honest here—change is hard!

CHANGE IS HARD

Even if we're not happy in the situation we're in, sometimes it feels easier to continue living the way we've been living than to make any attempt to do anything about it. Even if the way we're living now is wearing us down bit by bit, day by day, it can be hard to imagine life any other way. We can find ourselves thinking, consciously or unconsciously, *Well, if things could be different, they already would be.* Now, this doesn't make a whole lot of sense, of course, but deep down a lot of us hold this not-quite-sense-making belief without even realizing it!

Luckily, that's not true. Things *can* be different—things can always be different! No matter how long you've been stuck in the habits you've been stuck in, no matter how long you've been stuck with a particular feeling or a particular way of life, things can change. Starting today.

And the first step, the most important step to making that change is—I said it before and I'll say it again!— *imagine the life you want to live.*

This isn't a five-minute project. This is something to really consider. So set a time to meditate on it. Maybe right before you're going to sleep. Or first thing in the morning. Put your favorite music on and sit down with a notebook. And think about it. *Really* think about it. Don't be concerned if at first your answer is, "I don't know." Or if it takes a few days of really thinking about it to even begin to have the slightest bit of an idea.

When you think about it, try not to let yourself get too cluttered with other people's expectations and other people's dreams. And try not to be too influenced by the lives of celebrities. Imagine the life *you* want to live.

HERE ARE SOME QUESTIONS TO GET YOU STARTED

- How do I want to feel when I wake up each morning?

- How do I want to feel when I go to bed each night?

- What do I want my relationships with my friends to be like?

- What do I love to do?

- What's important to me?

- How do I most like to spend my time?

- What is valuable to me?

Think about the hierarchy of what is important in your life. And who is important. And how you would like to be spending your time.

If you find yourself getting really stuck, here's a fun exercise to try that might help. On a fresh sheet of notebook paper, write a few paragraphs describing the typical day of a made-up character—someone who is like you, but whom you might be mildly envious of if you met him/her. Someone whose life is *enough* like yours that it seems familiar, but different enough that you can imagine it as your goal. (Try not to make his/her life different from yours in areas that cannot at this time be changed—for example, if you live in Michigan, make your character live in Michigan. If you're five foot six, your character should be five foot six.) Describe his/her typical day. Write about him/her in the third person. Sometimes it is easier to imagine change when it's for a "him" not a "me." So we remove ourselves a little bit, and instead of thinking about the life we want, we imagine a life someone else might have. A life that we might like to have for ourselves.

If the life you're living now does not match the ideas you have in your head, don't panic! No matter how far you have to go, you can get there!

SCULPT YOUR LIFE

Here's another way to think about this question that might be helpful. It's based on a quote from Michelangelo. As you probably know, Michelangelo was an Italian Renaissance artist who was responsible for creating a lot of really famous pieces of art, including the ceiling of the Sistine Chapel and the statue of David, which may be the most famous sculpture of all time. Well, in addition to being an amazing artist, Michelangelo was also a pretty smart guy. He is quoted as having once said, "Every block of stone has a statue inside it, and it is the task of the sculptor to discover it."

This quote doesn't just apply to sculptures. It applies to life!

Imagine that *you* are the sculptor and the block of stone is your life. The life you want to live is a perfectly formed shape trapped inside that big old rock. Think of the clutter in your life—emotional, mental, and physical clutter—as chunks of stone clinging to the outside of that perfectly formed shape. It is already in there, ready, waiting for you. As I go forward, I will give you tools to help you chip away at all the extra things that are clinging to the life you want. The shape of your life is inside. Set it free!

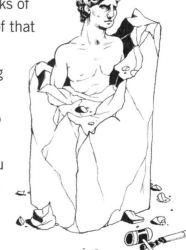

LET'S TALK ABOUT THE CLUTTER

CHAPTER SUMMARY . . .

There is only one main reason to declutter yourself—
because it will improve your life. No matter what your
goals are for yourself and your life, decluttering will
help you get there.

· ·

WHAT COMES NEXT . . .

In the next chapter we'll start thinking about the
living spaces that would best match the life you want
to live.

If you went into Heather McHavoc's room, you'd probably figure that she's obsessed with horses. In fact you'd be sure of it. Her walls are covered in horse posters. Her shelves are home to dozens of expensive horse figurines. Horse books fill her bookshelves, and horse magazines cover her desk. She even has horse bedsheets!

The problem? Heather isn't even that crazy about horses!

When she was a little kid, it's true, she did love horses. She read tons of horse books and thought she'd grow up and become a professional horseback rider. She requested horse figurines for every single birthday and holiday between the ages of five and twelve. Occasionally she would gallop around the house neighing. Once, when she was six, her parents caught her trying to ride the family dog around like a horse.

But as she got older, her tastes began to change. She still

likes horses, sure. And when she gets older, she still thinks it'd be cool to live on a ranch and own a couple of horses. However, now she's fourteen, and when she thinks about the life she wants to live, it's not 100 percent horsey 100 percent of the time. There's so much else out there!

For example, she just joined the swim team at her school. Despite the early morning practices (she wakes up at 5:45 a.m. on practice days—argh!) she really loves it. And after taking a few summer art classes, she realized she's actually quite a good painter. Who knew? She's also thinking about joining the Spanish club next year and maybe joining the staff of the school paper.

Only there's no room on her walls to display the yellow ribbons she's won at her first few swim meets (okay, no blues yet, but she's working up to one!). And there's no space in her room for her new easel, or her paints and brushes. Or anything else new. Why? Because her entire room is horse-horse-horse-horse-horse!

She'd love to get rid of some of the horse stuff, to make room for her new hobbies and interests. She'd also love to be able to invite her friends over without them referring to her room as "Heather's horse stable." (Yes, they just mean it as a joke, but they're kind of right!)

But what is she supposed to do with all the horse stuff?

CHAPTER 5

Reimagine the SWYKS

Now that you've begun to imagine the life you want to live, it's time to take that line of thinking one step further, and begin to think about the Spaces Where You Keep Stuff—your bedroom, your locker, your backpack, your shelf in the bathroom, etc.! (Going forward, we'll be referring to the Spaces Where You Keep Stuff as SWYKS—both because it's handy and because it's fun to say!) The SWYKS are a reflection of you. They say something about you, both to yourself and to others. They're a reflection of how you feel and how you see yourself. And, further, they *affect* how you feel and how you see yourself.

When you're trying to imagine your ideal spaces, when you're picturing the personal spaces that suit you best, try to imagine not only places that suit you *now* but places that suit the you who will be living the life you want. Remember the version of yourself that you wrote the paragraph about in the previous chapter—the version of yourself who is like you but just a few steps closer to living the life you'd ideally like to have? When you're imagining your ideal SWYKS, imagine them for *this* version of you. Or, to put it another way, if you'd like your life to be a little calmer, imagine what the SWYKS of a calmer person would look like. Perhaps they're decorated minimally in blues and greens, for example. Or if your ideal life is a little more exciting and energy-filled,

try to picture them decorated in bright, saturated tones of red and orange.

It might help to look through decorating magazines or at online decorating websites to get some ideas of what you like. When you find rooms that look similar to a room in which you'd like to live, write down a list of words that describe your ideal spaces. This list might include:

CALM SERENE **HaPPY** CHEERFUL
BRIGHT COLORFUL COZY **COOL**
SOOTHING O P e n **eARTHY**
DRAMATIC CReaTIVe**Fun**
THOUGHT-PROVOKING

Remember to keep the most important question in your mind: What is the life you want to lead? As we've discussed before, the life you live and the space in which you live are totally connected. The stuff you surround yourself with communicates important messages about who you are, both to other people and, even more importantly, to yourself! After all, the impression you make on other people is usually largely formed by how you think about yourself. And how you think about *yourself* is definitely affected by what you've chosen to surround yourself with.

Imagine that you had to keep a big bag of smelly garbage sitting in your room for a month. (Okay, I have no idea why you'd have to do this. Maybe you're storing it for a friend? Maybe you're in some sort of weird contest or you're on a reality show? Just go with

me here. . . .) How would this make you feel? Imagine what it would be like to come home every day and look at this big bag of gross garbage. Imagine how you'd eventually start to feel about yourself, just knowing it was in there. Your self-esteem might even start to suffer; you'd start to feel gross—dirty and depressed. Life would not seem very exciting. At the very least you'd be awfully relieved when, at the end of the month, the bag was taken away. Imagine how good it would feel when it was finally gone!

Why did I have you imagine that? Because your own clutter is an awful lot like this bag of smelly garbage. (Only for your sake—and your parents' sake, and your friends' sake!—let's hope it's less smelly.) It's still affecting how you feel every bit as much as this garbage would, even if you're not aware of it!

A NOTE ON PRACTICALITY

When I'm asking you to imagine your ideal living spaces, I'm not under some false assumption that you're living in an enormous mansion with thousands of dollars to spend on changing things. In fact I realize that almost everyone reading this book probably isn't. I realize that if you're like the vast majority of teenagers, you don't have a ton of money to spend, and you certainly don't have much of a say when it comes to certain aspects of your living situation—say, the size of your bedroom or the location of your house.

My intention in telling you to imagine your ideal living spaces is not to fill you with a sense of hopelessness about the space you have. When you're picturing your ideal room, it helps to remain somewhat realistic about it. While it might be fun to imagine having a 110-inch projection TV screen on your wall, or a diamond chandelier dangling from the ceiling, for most people this isn't terribly realistic. So when you're picturing your ideal living space, try to keep in mind the type of living space you could probably have *now*. Later we'll discuss how some significant changes can be made with very little money. And getting rid of clutter? Well, that costs nothing. And you might even end up making some money!

Once you picture your ideal room, it's time to open your eyes and look at your *actual* room, your actual backpack, your actual locker, your actual closet, etc., and ask yourself this question:

HOW FaR aRe YOU FROM WHeRe YOU WanT TO Be?

CHAPTER SUMMARY . . .

Looking at magazines and decorating websites is a great way to begin thinking about reimagining the SWYKS. But remember to stay practical when figuring out how you'd like to transform your spaces!

....

WHAT COMES NEXT . . .

In the next chapter we'll talk about "system overload" and figure out how bad your clutter actually is.

Caleb Clutterberg doesn't just like music, and he doesn't just love music. Music is Who He Is.

Why?

Well, it's probably in his genes. After all, he comes from a long line of the musically inclined. One of his grandmothers was an opera singer, and one of his grandfathers was a semifamous blues musician. His parents met when Caleb's dad came to see Caleb's mom's band eighteen years ago. One of his parents' favorite stories is about the time they put on a loud Kiss album and came into his room to make sure the music hadn't woken him up, and there was little Caleb, dancing, dancing, dancing right there in his crib with a huge smile on his face.

Now he's sixteen and music is everything to him. He loves downloading old blues songs and practicing playing guitar riffs right along with them. He's even in a band with two of his best friends. (They're called the Chaotics!) Every Sunday afternoon Caleb hits thrift stores and used record stores and garage sales looking for old records to add to his collection. Whenever he finds a record that 1) is by an artist he's heard of or 2) has a funny cover or 3) has a funny name or 4) is not too expensive, he snatches it up.

At last count Caleb had upwards of four thousand records. And he hasn't counted in an awfully long time. Some of the records aren't really anything he'd ever want to listen to. And some of the records aren't anything *anyone* would ever want to listen to, because they're too warped or scratched. But that's okay—they're part of his collection!

The only problem is this: As much as Caleb loves his records, lately it's starting to feel as though his collection is taking over his life. Records are sitting on his desk chair and lying on his desk. Records are on his bookshelves and on his nightstand and filling up the top three shelves of his closet. There are records blanketing the floor in stacks forty records high. The only place where you won't find records is his bed, and a very narrow path leading from his bed to his door.

Caleb has to do his homework at the kitchen table and can only practice guitar in the basement. He's only ever in his room to go to sleep, and he hasn't been able to have a friend over in a couple of years. After all, where would they go?

Sometimes Caleb doesn't even feel like his room is *his* room; he feels like he's a guest visiting a room that is lived in by his records.

CHAPTER 6

TAKING STOCK

It's hard to know how to fix a problem until you know what you're up against. So now it's time to look at how you are actually living and how that differs from how you'd like to be living. In this chapter we'll take a careful look at the SWYKS. We'll "take stock" and figure out how bad it actually is. But don't worry—no matter how cluttered you may be, no matter how far you are from where you'd like to get to, we'll get you there!

SYSTEM OVERLOAD

If your clutter system is *really* out of control, you may have reached what we call System Overload. System

Overload is a state of clutter so great that most of the items, spaces, and places in your life *no longer serve the purpose for which they were originally intended.* Maybe your bed is not providing you with a restful night's sleep. Your desk isn't a calm, organized place for you to do your homework. Your closet cannot hold all your clothes. Want to know if *you* are suffering from System Overload? Look at the list below and see how many of these items apply to you!

YOU KNOW YOU HAVE SYSTEM OVERLOAD . . .

- When you have to sleep curled up into a little ball because there is so much stuff on your bed.

- If you've ever had a nightmare that you were being attacked by any of the items in your room, only to wake up and find that you actually *were.*

- When the items in your closet are constantly falling off their hangers onto the floor of the closet, and you don't even bother trying to put them back on the hangers, because you know in a second they'll be back on the floor again. (Your closet is so overstuffed, your clothes are constantly fighting for space. For some reason your big mean winter coat is always picking on that sad outfit you wore to your cousin's wedding last year!)

- When you find yourself doing all your homework on your (bed, floor, toilet, kitchen table, parents' bed, insert-name-of-random-horizontal-surface-here) because your desk is too cluttered to use.

- When you constantly think you've lost your cell phone, keys, wallet, homework even though they're actually right there inside your very own backpack!

- When you find yourself carrying all your books around all day at school because there's no place to keep them in your locker.

- When you have to rearrange a bunch of items in the back or front seat of your car in order to make room for another human to sit there.

- When you get a new tube of toothpaste but can't fit it on your bathroom shelf because there are already six old half-used tubes of toothpaste stuck to it.

- When your TV has so much crap on top of it that you occasionally think your favorite show has a new character on it called Old Blue Shirt, until you realize that's actually your own old blue shirt ... dangling off the top of the TV!

If you checked off one item or more on this list, you're living with System Overload! Living with System Overload can be awfully stressful. Getting into a state of System Overload doesn't happen overnight. It usually occurs after weeks, months, or even years of letting our stuff pile up, clutter up, and take over!

EXTERNAL CLUTTER QUIZ

But maybe your clutter isn't quite that bad. Maybe you're not in System Overload, exactly; you just have a minor clutter problem. Or a medium-size clutter problem. If you want to find out what you're up against, take this quiz and find out:

HOW BAD IS IT?

1 Okay, you have five minutes to find your favorite shirt. Go!

A *Wait, only five minutes? Are you sure you don't mean fifty minutes? Because five minutes really isn't a very long time. And it's just, well, um . . . I know it's in here somewhere. I mean, I remember having seen it. It's just that I have so many shirts and . . . wait, is my time up already?*

B *Uh . . . I could do it in six for sure!*

C *Here it is.*

D *It's already hung up in my closet next to other shirts of a similar color/style. Do you want to see my second, third, and fourth favorite shirts also?*

2 Go stand in the middle of your room. How many individual items are on your floor that are not pieces of furniture?

A *How do you expect me to count that high? I'm not a professional mathematician!*

B *Ten-ish.*

C *Just a couple, two or three.*

D *Zero, unless my own feet count.*

3 What's under your bed?

A *I have no idea. Lost clothes? Shoes? Books? A turkey sandwich? It's been, uh, a while since I've checked. It's scary under there!*

B *Some stuff I stuck under there when I was "cleaning." I pretty much know what all of it is, though.*

C *Under-bed storage boxes with my stuff neatly organized inside. And maybe a dust bunny. Just one very lonely dust bunny. There are no friends for him under there, and he is quite small. Poor little guy.*

D *Wind.*

4 Does anything in your room require refrigeration, yet is not in the refrigerator?

A *I am DOING an EXPERIMENT, okay? Wasn't that how penicillin was created?*

B *No.*

C *No!*

D *No!!*

5 Your birthday was last week, and your friends and family gave you presents and cards. Where are they? What about the wrapping paper?

A *In the place of HONOR: on my floor, on my desk, and at the foot of my bed. And the wrapping paper is scattered in little bits all around the room because my cat got hold of it. But surely that isn't MY fault.*

B *The presents are all put away. The cards are in a pile on my desk. The wrapping paper is folded up next to the trash since I'm not sure if I want to save it and reuse it or not.*

C *Presents are put away. I'm saving the most special cards (i.e., the handmade one from my best friend and the one from my grandma) in a special box. The rest are in the process of being recycled. The wrapping paper is in the recycling bin.*

D *The presents are put away, except for two that I didn't care for. I'm donating that sweater to a local charity (when will my aunt realize I'm not a size two anymore?). And I'm returning the book my friend gave me (since I've already read it) and I'll use the gift receipt for something else. I'm saving one card in a scrapbook. The wrapping paper is being recycled.*

6 Unzip your book bag, stick your hand in, and grab the first item you touch. What is it?

A *Ew, I don't know. But I wish I'd been wearing gloves.*

B *A random piece of paper that was floating around in my bag. Actually, I think it was an assignment I was supposed to turn in last week but thought I'd lost. Oops!*

C *A water bottle, magazine, cell phone, or other nonschool item.*

D *My homework pad or datebook.*

7 Open your locker at school and what do you see?

A *THINGS FALLING OUT ON TO MY HEAD! OUCH.*

B *A tall tower of books, papers, notebooks, sports equipment, a comb, an iPod, etc. Okay, so there's a lot of stuff in here. But at least it's all balanced!*

C *Mostly stuff for school—notebooks and such. Also, a couple things for emergencies—like Band-Aids and duct tape. Gotta have duct tape! Also a couple pairs of flip-flops. I don't really know why those are there.*

D *A neat stack of stuff for school. A Band-Aid. A bright shiny apple.*

8 What percentage of the clothes in your closet do you actually wear?

A *Zero. The clothes in my closet are pretty much only stuff I don't actually wear. The stuff I do wear is in piles on the floor and over the back of my desk chair and under my bed. Y'know, so I can find them if I really need them.*

B *Hmm, I guess I have a lot of stuff in there that I don't wear. I use about 50 percent of what's in there.*

C *75 to 95 percent.*

D *95 to 100 percent.*

SCORING

Now tally up how many *A*s, *B*s, and *C*s you have, and consult the key below.

IF YOU CHOSE MOSTLY *A*s: Well, congratulations— you're a *Clutter King* or *Clutter Queen*! Only instead of a crown inlaid with a bunch of jewels and a castle full of servants, you get . . . A WHOLE LOT OF CRAP! So let's just put it this way: You have a lot of work ahead of you. But that's okay! When you're done, you're sure to experience a huge jump in happiness. Being this cluttered has almost surely been affecting many different areas of your life. You'll have some work to do going forward and some hard decisions to make. But won't you feel great when you have it all under control? Yes, you most certainly will!

IF YOU CHOSE MOSTLY *B*s: You're a *Resident of Clutter City*. You live in the land of clutter, and surely your clutter situation could be better, but it also could be worse! You definitely have some work ahead of you going forward. Good thing you're reading this book! You'll feel fantastic when you're done, and while it will surely take work to keep your clutter in order, I know you can do it!

IF YOU CHOSE MOSTLY *C*s: You're a *Visitor to Clutter City*. Not a constant visitor, but certainly a regular one. And every time you're there, you probably pick up a few cluttery souvenirs. But just a few. You've done a pretty good job keeping the clutter from getting too crazy, but surely it is affecting your life to some extent. All clutter does! You can surely benefit from some decluttering. Really, who couldn't?

IF YOU CHOSE MOSTLY *D*s: *You Have Moved Far Away from the Land of Clutter.* Your clutter situation is pretty under control. You don't live in Clutter City or even any of the surrounding areas! That's great! Maybe you're a naturally organized person, or maybe you've just recently done a big overhaul. But just keep in mind, Clutter City is the type of place that can easily pull a person back in!

ARE YOU A GUEST IN THE HOME OF YOUR STUFF?

Sometimes, without meaning to, people forget that their possessions are meant to be tools. Everything you own is a tool of some kind, intended to serve some purpose to benefit or enrich your life. Your bed is a tool that helps you sleep; your photos of your friends are a tool to help you feel loved and to make you smile; your desk is a tool that helps you do your homework; your clothes are tools that keep you from being naked! But sometimes when we forget that our stuff is supposed to serve us, we start to believe that we are supposed to serve our stuff. Did you see that movie *Fight Club*? Remember that famous quote? "The things you own end up owning you." Well, that happens more often than we might like to think. Far too often the stuff that's supposed to help us takes over and starts running the show. In the pie of life, the stuff is getting the best piece and leaving us with only crumbs!

Suddenly our stuff gets the best seat at the table and the most comfortable spot on the couch. Our stuff blocks our view out the window and makes our SWYKS stressful and unusable. Suddenly it's as though *we* are guests in the house of our stuff. Only we can't just go home, because we're already there! What we need to do is send our stuff packing. But it's not easy.

Once the stuff has taken over, it becomes awfully hard to get rid of. We find ourselves making up a ton of excuses as to why the stuff can't leave, why the stuff should get to stay and ruin our lives. *It's valuable! It's precious! It's important!* we say. But are *we* really saying this? Or have we been brainwashed by the stuff? In the next chapter we'll discuss some of the biggest hurdles we have to getting out from under our clutter problem. And then it's time to start finding solutions!

CHAPTER SUMMARY . . .

If you take just one thing away from this chapter, I hope it's this: Everything you own is a tool of some kind, intended to serve some purpose to benefit or enrich your life. If your stuff isn't working *for* you, it's time to let it go!

....

WHAT COMES NEXT . . .

There are tons of reasons why people hold on to stuff that they don't actually want or use or need. In the next chapter we'll talk about some of the hurdles people have when it comes to getting rid of clutter. And for every hurdle, we'll discuss how to leap right over it into the wondrous land of the clutter-free.

Fifteen-year-old José Hoardez and his nineteen-year-
old brother, Jason, have always been great friends. Jason
is a full three and a half years older, but even when
they were kids, Jason never treated José like some little
tagalong kid brother. Jason always just treated José like
a buddy, an equal . . . an equal who just so happened to
be shorter and not allowed to do as much stuff, but still.
It didn't matter: They were team J-squared.

For example: When Jason was ten, he and his friends
started getting into climbing the trees behind their

house, and Jason always let José come along and never made fun of him when he occasionally needed a boost to reach those high-up branches. (Occasionally Jason's friends would try to tease José about this, but Jason always told them to shut up.) A couple of years after that, when Jason got a video game system for his birthday, he let José play every game and taught him all the cheat codes. And last year, when José started at the high school where Jason was a senior, Jason gave José rides to school every day. Even on Tuesdays, when Jason had first period free and could have slept forty-five minutes later. Jason gave up *sleep* for him. And Jason *loves* to sleep!

Jason has always been really into computers. Starting when he was thirteen (and José was nine), Jason earned extra money by taking old computers people were throwing away and using the parts to build new computers, which he then sold. Jason is kind of a computer genius. He made so much money he was able to buy himself a used convertible, and he started giving both of them rides to school in that with the top down. It was pretty awesome.

But then at the end of last year something terrible happened—Jason graduated high school and started getting ready to go to college five hundred miles away! A few days before he left, Jason packed as much of his stuff as he could fit in that pretty darn awesome convertible—just the stuff he'd need for school. He knew his mom wanted to turn his bedroom into a guest room (which he was totally cool with), so he decided he'd just recycle all the stuff that wouldn't fit in the backseat or the trunk. The pile of stuff he was getting rid of was basically just a bunch of computer parts he'd gotten for free and a few computer books that he'd already read.

But as soon as José saw that Jason was planning to do this, José said no way! "You should just keep all your old stuff in my room," José said. "I'll keep it for you!"

Jason protested, said this wasn't necessary. But José insisted. "You might need it one day!" he said. But the truth was, José thought the idea of Jason getting rid of all this stuff was just too sad. Their house was going to be empty enough without Jason there. If his computer stuff wasn't lying around, it'd be like he'd never been there at all.

José carried Jason's leftover stuff into his room. It took three trips.

That was six months ago. And for the last six months José has been living in what looks like a computer repair shop that was ransacked and then hit by a hurricane. Everywhere José looks, there's an old monitor staring at him. Or a book on a computer language José doesn't speak. And at least three times a day he steps on some miscellaneous pointy computer thingy. And that really hurts!

José's mom keeps nagging him to clean up his room and get rid of all this stuff. "You don't need it!" she says. But José just shakes his head. He does need it. He needs to save it. For Jason! Just in case . . . right?

CHAPTER 7

HURDLES!

As a professional organizer I have been called into hundreds of people's houses to help them get organized. I've been to all types of homes —giant mansions and tiny cottages. Three-story houses in the suburbs and one-room apartments in the city. I've gone into homes where eight people live and houses occupied by just a single, very cluttered person. But despite how different the houses and locations have been, the residents of these homes have all had at least two very important things in common: They all have clutter (well, obviously, or I wouldn't be there), and they have lots of "very good reasons" why their clutter needs to stay.

No matter how overwhelmed their clutter makes them feel. No matter how much their clutter is making them miserable. No matter how hard it is to live in a cluttery home, everyone who is cluttered is filled with excuses, excuses, excuses.

But there's something I need to tell you. You, right there, sitting reading this book—no matter what reasons you have for keeping your clutter, they are wrong. No matter how much you think you may desperately need all of it, you are wrong. I'm not trying to be a jerk when I say this. I have nothing but sympathy for people whose own excuses have trapped them in situations they're not happy in. But the truth is, I will say it again: YOUR REASONS ARE WRONG!

There is nothing more important than your happiness. *And clutter steals happiness.*

And further, almost all of these excuses are based on misconceptions of some kind—about the stuff in your life, what it can do, what it *should* do. And most of these misconceptions are formed by the fact that here today in America we have a kind of wacky, dysfunctional relationship with our stuff.

What do I mean by dysfunctional? I mean a relationship that is not working. The very fact that you have clutter and are reading this book proves this. And by this I do not mean to say that everything that is cluttering the SWYKS now needs to be given away, sold, or simply tossed. But I do mean that as soon as something becomes "clutter," it's no longer doing anything good for you. Here are some of the most common excuses I've heard. See if you can recognize yours:

EHCUSES, EHCUSES

EHCUSE I:

> But this stuff is valuable!

This is one of the most common, if not *the* most common, excuses I hear from my clients. I hear it from teens, adults, everyone! And I get it —I absolutely do. Recent economic events have made money especially tight for just about everyone. And these facts make this one of the hardest excuses to get around.

Maybe you have an after-school job at the local bookstore, or maybe you babysit on weekends. Maybe you work at a coffee shop or do odd jobs for your neighbors. Or maybe you get an allowance from your parents, for which you're expected to do a bunch of extra chores around the house. Or maybe you only get money for holidays and birthdays and have to ration that out all year. Whatever your situation, chances are you don't have unlimited access to funds. And therefore, when you paid good money for something (or even when someone else has spent money on something), even if it is something you never used in the first place or will never use again, you don't want to just get rid of it.

So what if that broken iPod makes all songs sound like they're being played underwater, and you already got a new one for your birthday? You'll get that old one fixed and sell it, right? And okay, so that shirt you bought six months ago didn't look that good once you got home and cut the tags off (damn those dressing room mirrors!), but maybe one day it will look good somehow, right? And what about that book you bought two years ago but only read half of because it was really boring? You might go back to it one day. Y'know, when you run out of other things to read. And what about those Rollerblades you thought you'd use all the time that now just sit by your bedroom door, sad and neglected, waiting to trip you? Or the trumpet you bought on eBay when you thought you might learn to play trumpet (before you realized that playing trumpet is *very hard*) that is now just functioning as a slightly rusty trumpet-shaped sculpture at the back of your closet? You should hang on to these things because they're worth valuable money, right?

WRONG, WRONG, WRONG, WRONG, WRONG!

Because we put so much emphasis on money, it is easy to forget that money isn't the only thing that has value. Your time has value. Your happiness has value. Just because you can't put a price tag on how good it feels to be clutter-free doesn't mean it's not worth something. It's worth a lot! And I would argue it's worth a lot more than any random item floating around your room.

Now, I'm not telling you to throw everything away; I'm just asking you to be realistic when you're thinking about the best way to get rid of a particular item. If you really want to fix your old iPod and sell it, ask yourself some serious questions: *When* exactly are you going to do it? And who is going to buy it? Have you looked online and seen what a used iPod costs? And is this cost high enough to justify the time (and money) it would take you to fix it, list it, sell it, and ship it? If the answer is yes, then pick a date, a *specific date* by which you are going to have this all done. Don't make it more than two weeks in the future. And if the answer is no? Then you need to get rid of it!

Sometimes you just need to cut your losses. Your time is valuable. Even if you don't pay yourself by the hour just for being alive, every hour you are alive on this earth is worth something. And your happiness is valuable. Even if you can't put a dollar amount on it, it is worth an awful lot more than that iPod or that ugly shirt is. And clutter steals happiness. It is a fact. It just does. So getting rid of your excess clutter is the price you pay to buy back your space, and buy back your life!

EHCUSe 2:

> I don't have time to deal with all of this stuff.

This one is another biggie. I know, I know, I just said how valuable your time is. And with school and after-school activities and homework and family responsibilities, you probably don't have a ton of free time, so why would you want to spend it getting rid of your junk? After all, cleaning and organizing are probably not on your Top Ten List of Fun Things to Do. They might not even be on your Top One Hundred List. Or One Thousand! But I'll tell you what—no matter how busy you are, you *do* have time. And the time you spend now getting rid of your crap will come back to you times ten.

Clutter not only robs us of space and happiness, but it makes us less productive. We spend valuable time sorting through the clutter looking for things we need. And just being *around* clutter slows us down. Even if you can't devote an entire weekend to getting the SWYKS in order, you can surely devote an hour, half an hour, or even fifteen minutes a day to getting rid of your excess stuff. Don't just wait until you have free time: Set a time and schedule the rest of your life around it.

EHCUSE 3:

I might need it one day.

In terms of excuses, this is another gigantic one. Pretty much every house I've ever gone into for the purpose of decluttering is piled high with stuff that's being saved "for the future." And I have seen people save some pretty silly stuff: Seventy-three rolls of paper towels, forty-eight pairs of unworn socks, twenty-two identical T-shirts, five hundred Ping-Pong balls. (I wanted to ask the owner of all these balls, "What sort of future could you possibly be imagining in which you could need this many Ping-Pong balls?")

I'll be the first to admit that planning for the future is important. One day you will move out of your parents' home. You will go to college; you will get a job. The rest of your life is ahead of you, and the truth is that you don't know, you *can't* know what it will hold. This is an exciting thing, but it can also be an unsettling thing. I mean, you want things to go well; you want to be prepared. This is understandable.

But saving stuff you don't need now and might never need is not the way. Some people hold on to stuff "just in case," as though having all this stuff is going to protect them from some of the uncertainty life can bring. The truth is, though, it won't. No one is more and better prepared for the future just by having twenty-seven blank sheets of poster board. I am not saying you shouldn't think about the future; what I am saying is that one of the best ways to prepare is to be fully alive in the present. To live *now*, and experience *now*. And know that when the future comes, *whatever it holds*, you'll handle it.

EHCUSE 4:

It reminds me of the past.

As tempting as it is to stockpile for an unknown future, it is also tempting to try to hang on to the past by keeping a bunch of stuff around that reminds us of it. The thing is, you're not a kid anymore. And as much as you might have loved (or hated) being a kid, a lot of the things you once owned probably don't really fit your life now. That princess bed or those spaceship sheets you used to love don't seem so cool anymore. You're too embarrassed about your dinosaur wallpaper to invite

your crush over to study. And all those ballerina dolls that were once prominently displayed in the center of your room are now pirouetting in a messy pile under your bed, because you don't want anyone to see them.

But then, what are you supposed to *do* with all that stuff?

I'm not trying to tell you to toss your entire childhood. Keeping a few reminders of days gone by can be a nice way to honor the past. But problems arise when we attach so much meaning to the *objects* that we confuse them with the experience. That T-shirt you got with your best friend last year when you went with his family to Maryland might remind you of the experience, but *it is not the experience itself.*

Mistaking "things" for "experiences" is one way in which so many of us have a dysfunctional relationship with our stuff.

If you never wear that "I Got Crabby in Maryland" shirt, you don't have to keep it just to remind yourself that the trip happened. When you've had an experience, no one can erase it, whether you have mementos from it or not. I'm not saying you shouldn't save old photos, or T-shirts, or notes. I'm just saying you shouldn't give these items more meaning than they deserve. Or more space than they deserve. A T-shirt is always just a T-shirt, no matter who wore it or who gave it to you or where you got it.

If you can't bear to part with that shirt, consider taking a photograph of it, and perhaps framing a few pictures of you and your friend on this trip (along with a picture of the shirt) and putting it up on your wall.

But remember, while thinking about the future and the past are worthwhile things to do, you only live in the present, and the more thought, time, and energy you devote to that, the happier you'll be.

EXCUSE 5:

But this stuff is useful. Getting rid of it would be a waste!

Many of us were brought up being taught not to waste things, so we feel guilty and like we're doing something "bad" if we get rid of something that someone might find useful. I was brought up this way too, so I definitely understand. But there are plenty, *plenty*, of things you can do with your items other than just feed them to the garbage.

YOU CAN:

- **DONATE** items that are in good shape to a homeless shelter or a thrift store. Search online to find different charities in your neighborhood that accept donations. Some charities will even send a truck by your house to pick up your items!

- **SELL** items on eBay or have a garage sale. This can be a fun thing to do as well as a good way to earn extra money. Just don't let *planning* the sale take up too much of your time and your life. If you're decluttering in winter, scrap the garage sale idea, unless you live somewhere where it's warm all year long. If you're planning on selling items on eBay, do a search and see how much similar items are fetching, so you'll know whether it's worth your time or not. Remember, your time is the most valuable thing you have!

- **GIVE** items to your friends. (But only if you think they'll really use them. Don't force your friends to deal with your clutter!)

And if no one wants your used items? Recycle, recycle, recycle! So many things can be recycled these days. You can look online to see what can be recycled in your neighborhood.

EHCUSE 6:

It was a gift.

No matter how well our friends and family know us, sometimes we will be given something we don't want. It can be tricky to navigate the waters of the unwanted gift. You love your family and friends and don't want to hurt their feelings. And of course hurting feelings should be avoided when possible. But being kind to the people we love does not and should not require that we wear itchy stuff or hang disturbing evil clown paintings up in our rooms!

Occasionally, you or your parents might want you to keep a specific item—a handmade sweater knit by your aunt Louise, for example. You don't wear it, but you know it actually would genuinely hurt her feelings if she thought you'd gotten rid of it. In certain very special circumstances you might need to keep something you do not want, to preserve the peace and keep from hurting someone's feelings. And this is fine. But this is the exception—not the rule.

You cannot necessarily do anything about gifts you've already received, but in the future it is certainly fair to ask *not* to be given items. Just make sure you explain gently and kindly to the people in your life that while you appreciate that they want to give you gifts and while you've certainly appreciated all the gifts they've given you in the past, you are trying to have less stuff in your life (even very nice stuff like the gifts they've given you!). And that in the future you'd love it if any gifts could be given in the form of an experience instead of an actual item.

You can make an effort to give these types of gifts too. Gifts of experience can include—a trip to a favorite restaurant, or a trip to see a band or a play. A one-day membership to a local health club or swimming pool. A manicure or some other luxury service. Bake your best friend his favorite kind of cake, or write a short story for your best friend starring the two of you.

Gifts of experience not only prevent your clutter pile from growing bigger, but they are some of the most memorable and meaningful presents you can give or receive. Do I remember every single item I got for my eleventh birthday? No, I don't remember a single one of them. But do I remember the fact that one of my older brothers volunteered to do all of my chores for me for two entire weeks as a birthday gift? Absolutely. This is something I doubt I will ever forget.

I know one family who *never* gives each other presents for any of their occasions—Christmas, birthdays, etc. Instead they save all of the money they would have spent on each other in a special savings account, and at the end of the year they go on a trip. Last year they spent an entire week at the beach with all the money they saved!

EXCUSE 7:

I can't deal with any of this! Ack! It's all too overwhelming!

Yes, the process of not only getting rid of a ton of clutter but also changing your relationship with the stuff in your life can seem overwhelming at first. I hear you! I really do! I will be the first to admit that this process is hard.

But you know what's even harder? Living every day with a bunch of crap. Even if it *seems* like you're saving yourself distress by not dealing with your clutter, you're not. Every day you spend in a cluttery space is a day that you're not fully getting to live. I know, this might sound a little dramatic, but it's true.

Okay, imagine this: You have a bad cold— a very stuffy nose, which makes it hard to breathe. Isn't it hard to be in a good mood when your nose is all stuffed up? When you can't quite breathe freely and easily? Of course it is. And the clutter in your life is clogging you as much as a bunch of snot is. Look, I'm not trying to be gross here, but you have to face the facts, people! As overwhelming as it can be to deal with all of this, once you do, you will feel such joy and relief that it will make it all worth it. Every last bit of the work you did will absolutely be worth it.

So don't panic! In the coming chapters we're going to go through the decluttering process step by step, and each of these steps will be relatively easy to do. We'll also discuss the importance of starting small, seeking help, and breaking it all down into manageable steps.

EXCUSE 8:

But it's part of my collection.

Comic books, baseball cards, mugs, spoons, hats, giant pens, tiny bottles of hotel shower gel, state quarters, wheat pennies, Sharpie markers, dolls, stamps, tea kettles, stuffed animals, items with pictures of cows on them, items with pictures of frogs on them, Hello Kitty merchandise, *Star Wars* action figures, miniatures, shoelaces, wristbands, DVDs, old magazines, old postcards, old photographs of other people's families, old slides, nonworking cameras, VHS tapes, soda cans from other countries, foreign coins—in all my years of visiting people's homes I have become convinced that if an item exists, there is someone who collects it.

But just because you're calling something a "collection" does not mean you have to keep it forever.

I'm not trying to say there is something wrong with having a collection of some kind. And if you're treating your collection of avocado pits with respect—displaying them in a special display case or something—and you actually have room for them, then by all means, collect away! Collecting something can be fun. But if your collection is tucked away in a drawer somewhere, or in a box under your bed, or shoved in the back of a closet covered in dust, then, really, what's the point?

Collecting something for the sake of collecting something doesn't make a whole lot of sense. I know you might be thinking, "But what if it's worth money someday?" And maybe you've even heard one of those "horror" stories about someone whose parents threw out their comic book collection, and *if only* they still had it, it would be worth thousands of dollars. But for every story like that there are tens of thousands more stories about people who got rid of a bunch of old junk and never even missed it for a second.

EXCUSE 9:

But it belongs to
someone else.

It's awfully easy to end up cluttered with a bunch of other people's stuff—your friend asks you to hold her sweatshirt in your backpack because hers is full; your little sister leaves a bunch of her coloring books on your floor; you have a sleepover and someone forgets to take their pillow home.

It's easy to end up with a bunch of other people's stuff; what's hard is getting rid of it!

It's not your stuff, so you don't want to just recycle it, sell it, donate it, or throw it away. But at the same time you don't want it in the SWYKS anymore, and it can be hard to get your friends to take it all back. Sometimes you might have some stuff in your room and not even know whose stuff you have! But you should not let someone else's clutter be stealing your space.

So here's what I suggest: A week or two before you start on a big decluttering, make a list of all the stuff that's cluttering up your spaces that is not yours.

Collect everything together, lay it all out on your floor, and take a picture. Then e-mail the list and the picture attachment to everyone who might possibly own one of these items, along with this note: *Dearest Friends, I am in the process of getting rid of clutter. Is any of this stuff yours? If so, please claim it ASAP. I love you, but ten days from today I will be putting all unclaimed items on my front lawn and lighting them on fire. Thanks! Love, (your name goes here).* Okay, so you're not actually going to light their stuff on fire (seriously, I am not advocating lighting stuff on fire!), but if they don't claim it in ten days, what you're actually going to do is donate all the stuff to a local charity. But there's nothing like the threat of a favorite sweater/hat/pillow burning on your front lawn to inspire your friends to come take their stuff back!

Oh, and if it's something you've borrowed from a friend, not something they've left in one of the SWYKS, it might be nicer just to bring it back to them and say thanks.

EXCUSE 10:

But my stuff represents who I am!

How do you think about yourself? How would you like others to think of you? Are you creative? Artsy? Musical? Sporty? Alternative? Studious? Do you ever feel like you have to own certain items to prove that you belong to a certain group? Well, if you do, you're surely not alone. But you're also surely not right.

Despite what advertisers might have you believe, *you are not your stuff!*

Okay, on one level I am so sure you already know this. But this message is delivered to us, to *all* of us, over and over—on billboards and in television commercials and print ads and ads online. And if we're not consciously *weeding out* this message, it's easy to absorb it and just accept the idea that we have to own certain items in order to prove to others (and ourselves) that we are who we are.

Except that it's completely false!

If you're a creative person, you are a creative person *whether or not* your room is filled with dried-up tubes of paint. And hanging on to ten pairs of old cleats that are far too worn (and smelly) to wear doesn't make you a more serious baseball player than the person who only has one pair. And if you're a music lover, having ten thousand CDs you don't listen to doesn't make you more of one. Hanging on to stuff that you don't actually use just makes you a person with less space and more clutter. Your identity is not dependent on what you own. It never was, and it never will be.

EXCUSE II:

But I just don't have enough space.

I've heard this excuse over and over, and I'm sorry to tell you, but you won't convince me with this one. The problem is *not* that you don't have enough space; it's that you have too much stuff! You might *like* to have more space. You might feel like you *need* more space, but the amount of space you have is the amount of space you have. I know, it sucks to not have room to keep all the stuff you want to keep. But whether it's fair or not, the space you have is the space you have. So until you invent a stuff-shrinking laser gun or a room-expanding laser gun, only a certain amount of stuff is going to be able to reasonably fit in it. And unfortunately, what fits where is determined by simple math and physics, not by how much you might want to cram it all in.

Look, if you think you'll be able to convince your parents to get a brand-new wing stuck onto your house so you'll have somewhere to keep your sizeable cartoon character sleeping bag collection and all those framed inspirational kitten posters, then by all means keep all your stuff! But if not, then it all comes down to this: If you have more stuff than you have space, the *only* way to get clutter-free is to get rid of some of it. No matter how much you might feel like you "need" all of it, no matter how much you might feel like you can't live without it, you'll live a happier, calmer, less stressful, more productive life in a room that contains only as much stuff as there's room for.

EXCUSE 12:

But I don't really mind the mess!

Okay, I'm not going to try to convince you that you hate mess if you truly believe you love it. But let me just mention that being accustomed to living a certain way or being used to a particular situation is not the same thing as actually liking it. Or being happy with it. You might *think* you don't mind the mess because you're used to living with it. But even if you're not aware of the ways in which it bothers you, I can almost guarantee you it does.

I said it before and I'll say it again: Change. Is. Hard! All kinds of change: bad change, neutral change, good change. All of it is hard! Sometimes people try to convince themselves that they don't mind a particular situation because it's easier than having to admit to themselves that they don't like it. After all, it's a lot easier to justify not doing something about a perfectly fine situation than it is to justify not doing something about a situation that is actually taking away from your life. To put it another way, if one admits one doesn't like something, then one has no excuse not to change it. And who has time and energy for all this changing?

But don't trick yourself into thinking you don't mind something just because changing it'll be hard. No matter how much effort it takes to get rid of your clutter, it will absolutely be worth it in the end. I guarantee it!

The longer you've lived with mess and clutter, the less you're going to be aware of its effect on you and your life. But that doesn't mean it's not affecting you. In fact, exactly the opposite. The longer you've lived with the clutter, the further-reaching its effects may be. The good news is, the more your clutter has been stealing from your life, the greater sense of relief you'll have when you finally get rid of it.

HERE ARE SOME ADDITIONAL QUESTIONS TO CONSIDER WHEN EVALUATING THE IMPACT OF YOUR CLUTTER

- How is my clutter affecting my emotions and relationships?

- How is my clutter affecting my family and friends?

- How is my clutter affecting the way I react to things?

- How is my clutter preventing me from living the life I want to live?

THE MEMORY GAME

This simple game is a good way
to get into the decluttering mind-
set. So get out a few sheets of
paper and a pen (or better yet
turn on your computer so you're
not making extra paper clutter
for yourself) and a clock or

stopwatch (your cell phone probably has one). At the
top of each sheet write down the name of a major
SWYKS: bedroom, bathroom shelf, backpack, locker,
etc. (If you have your own car, or store a lot of stuff
in whatever car you most frequently travel in, you'll
want to make a sheet for this, too.)

Here's how to play: Pick a SWYKS and then set
your timer for three minutes. For the next three
minutes try to remember every single item that's
in one particular SWYKS. (Don't cheat! It might be
helpful to do this game in a room other than your
bedroom.) At the end of three minutes move onto
the next SWYKS. Do this until you've devoted three
minutes to remembering and listing every item in
each SWYKS.

Now, when you've completed your lists, go check
out your actual SWYKS and see how well you did.
Did you forget that you have five old copies of *Us*

Weekly on your nightstand? Did you forget that you're keeping three extra pairs of flip-flops in a pile at the back of your closet? Look at the items you forgot to list, and ask yourself this question:

IF I CAN'T even REMEMBER THAT I OWN SOMETHING, DO I ACTUALLY NEED IT?

LET'S TALK ABOUT THE CLUTTER

CHAPTER SUMMARY . . .

No matter what your reasons are for hanging on to your clutter, there's an even better reason for getting rid of it: Getting rid of clutter will improve your life!

WHAT COMES NEXT . . .

In the next chapter we'll talk about what happens when your clutter intersects with the clutter belonging to the other people in your life. We'll also figure out your clutter communication type.

Sixteen-year-old Tessa and Jessa Messerton are identical twins, but they couldn't be more different.

Jessa loves sports (baseball in the spring and basketball in the winter) and animals (their family has a dog and three cats, all of which she rescued from the shelter) and is learning to make her own clothes. Her room is filled with sports equipment, cat toys, and a dog bed, as well as tons and tons of pieces of fabric, ribbons, and an old tabletop sewing machine that she got at a garage sale six months ago. So far she's made three cute dresses and five cute skirts.

Tessa loves clothes too. Except that Tessa's tastes run more toward the premade kind of clothes. The ones with fancy brand-name labels. Tessa also loves acting in and writing plays. Her room is filled with costumes and scripts, clothes and makeup. And a large number of teeny-tiny cactuses in little decorative pots.

Tessa and Jessa love each other, sure, but lately it's hard to imagine they shared a space in the same womb for nine months without killing each other. Well, actually, they were only in there for eight and a half months; they came out two weeks early. . . . No wonder—they drive each other crazy!

And speaking of driving . . . that is sort of the problem. See, up until a few months ago, Jessa and Tessa got along pretty well. But then they turned sixteen. And the day after their sixteenth birthday they both got their driver's licenses. They both wanted cars, but neither had enough to afford one on her own, so they pooled all their savings, and with a little bit of help from their parents they bought a car to share.

Only the problem is—their car is so cluttered with their collective crap it is making them both miserable. The trunk, the backseat, and even the cup holders are packed with an insane collection of pieces from both of their lives: costumes, magazines, makeup, sports equipment, scripts, a dog bed, cat toys, and a few crushed doggie treats from when they spilled on the floor of the car and neither one of them ever cleaned them up. Their car is so messy that they both feel stressed as soon as they get in. And while they'd love to be able to give their friends rides sometimes, there'd be nowhere for them to sit! Neither Tessa nor Jessa wants to clean it up, since each is convinced it's the other one's mess. Their friends and family have jokingly (well, semijokingly) started referring to it as the Mess Mobile. The name fits!

But really, the whole thing isn't very funny. Their messy car is not only ruining their relationship with each other, but it's making things tense for their entire family. Their parents say they regret helping them buy the car, since they've done pretty much nothing but fight ever since they got it.

CHAPTER 8

YOUR CLUTTER

and THE PEOPLE In YOUR LIFE

In an ideal world we would all have plenty of space to keep all of our stuff. And in an ideal world our clutter wouldn't ever have to affect anyone else's well-being. And, hey, in an ideal world we would all be able to fly around without airplanes and shoot magic rainbow rays out of our fingertips. But the world we live in is not the ideal world; it is the real world. And the truth is, our stuff not only affects us, it affects our family and friends and everyone we come in contact with. (And magic rainbow rays probably won't be invented for at least another few hundred years.)

Relationships are hard, especially relationships with the people you live with. You're around each other

when you're at your best and at your worst, when you feel like being around people and when you don't. Those things alone make getting along tricky, but then add a whole bunch of clutter into the mix, and . . . well, it's no wonder families who live in clutter often find themselves in near constant fights, with the clutter as both the background and a source.

But simply clearing out our space won't stop the clutter from trying to creep back into our emotional, physical, and mental spaces. So it's important not only to imagine the life we want and try to adjust our outside life to fit, but to think about how we communicate about our clutter with the people we live with.

And we're not just talking physical clutter—we're talking mental clutter and emotional clutter as well. The quiz on the next page will help get you thinking about your clutter, the clutter of those in your household, and your clutter communication type.

CLUTTER COMMUNICATION QUIZ

WHAT'S YOUR TYPE?

It's Saturday. You have two midterms next week, a biology project due on Thursday, and a huge basketball game tomorrow. You're so overwhelmed your head is about to explode, and your mom has just asked you if you wouldn't mind watching your little sister for the afternoon when you were planning to study. This is not the first time this has happened. What do you do?

A *Calmly ask if there is anyone else who can watch li'l sis, because you have a ton of studying to do. If the answer is yes, great! If not, you'll suck it up this one last time. Later, discuss with your mom the possibility of finding a regular babysitter for your sister on days when you and she are both particularly busy.*

B *Tell your mom this is completely unfair. This happens all the time. Does she want you to fail? Lose your temper. Then storm out of the room.*

C *Sigh very heavily and then agree to watch your sister. Look as world-weary as possible. Sigh very heavily again. Wait for someone to commend you for your heroism. Get very upset when no one does.*

D *Agree, and then put your sister to work cutting out pictures of DNA for your bio poster. After all, she did get an A-plus in scissor skills! Or, barring that, plop her in front of Wall-E. She can't get enough of that guy.*

E *Watch your sister, but don't get any work done. Decide to pretend there are no such things as midterms or projects. At least not for now. You will deal with all of this later!*

2 **Your older brother has piled up seemingly every single one of his possessions in the middle of the living room, and in only twenty minutes your three best friends are supposed to come over and watch *American Idol*. What do you do?**

A *Say, "Hey, bro, my besties are coming over in twenty minutes. I know it's your living room too, but if you could help me clean up your stuff really fast, I will totally owe you one."*

B *Shout, "I cannot believe you are taking over the living room again! Am I ever allowed to use this room? It's the* family *room, you know. Do you even know? Or do you think it's just yours now?"*

C *Don't say anything. Go into the room and sigh. Hope your brother notices how much you want him to clean up. Sit in the living room until your friends get there. When they come inside, apologize profusely, loudly, for the mess. Accidentally intentionally stub your toe on one of his barbells. Shake your head while sighing.*

D *What do I do about what? Oh, you mean the mess? What mess? I don't even see any mess!*

E *Collect all his stuff and put it in neat piles in front of his bedroom door.*

3 You're doing a big school project on the dining room table (you need a clean space, and your desk is a mess). Your younger brother has just started taking your stuff off the table and tossing it onto the couch because your mom said he's supposed to set the table for dinner. What do you do?

A *Very nicely ask your mom if it would be possible for the family to have dinner in the kitchen tonight, just this once, so that you can finish your project.*

B *Shout, "WHAT THE HECK ARE YOU DOING?!?! I AM WORKING HERE! MOM, WHY ARE YOU TELLING HIM TO MOVE MY STUFF?!"*

C *Let your brother move all of your stuff onto the couch. Don't help him, but don't stop him. Secretly hope he ruins your project so that you can be annoyed about it.*

D *Take your stuff off the table yourself. Bring it into your room. Take everything off your desk and move it onto the floor just so you can finish the project. Vow to find a better place for all that stuff the second you're done with your work.*

E *Let your brother toss your project onto the couch. Help him set the table. Maybe you'll finish your project later or something.*

4 You just got a brand-new bike, but your family's garage is so full of clutter that you truly cannot find a space for it. What do you do?

A *Wait until dinnertime, and then while everyone is eating, ask when would be a good time to schedule a big family decluttering of the garage.*

B *Stand in the garage and scream, "HELLO, I LIVE HERE TOO, AND THERE IS NO ROOM FOR MY BIKE!"*

C *Stuff your bike on top of the clutter and slam the door.*

D *Spend the entire day cleaning out the garage yourself.*

E *Leave your bike outside on the front lawn. So what if it's raining? Rust looks cool, right?*

5 Nothing is going right today! Your parents are mad at you for failing a test, your older sister is mad at you for taking too long in the bathroom this morning, your best friend just snapped at you for unknown reasons, and your dog, Woofie, just made a delicious snack out of your favorite shoe. What do you do?

A Explain to your parents that you did the best you could and you'll study harder next time. Make a morning bathroom schedule with your sister. Ask your best friend what's going on. Tell Woofie to stop eating your shoes and then run around with him in the backyard for a while until you both feel better.

B Scream, "WOOFIE, I CANNOT BELIEVE YOU ATE MY SHOE!" and then storm out of the room.

C Apologize to everyone, but in such a way that they know you actually feel very hurt and perhaps did not do anything wrong. Wait for them to apologize to you.

D Tell your parents you'll study harder next time. Plan a time to talk to your best friend and see what's up. Write out a bathroom schedule for you and your sister to follow on weekdays so that you won't always be stepping over each other in the mornings. Vow to keep all your shoes in your closet with the door closed.

E Go in your room. Close the door. Lie down. Take a nap. Hear Woofie chewing on more of your shoes while you sleep. Ignore it.

Tally up how many *A*s, *B*s, *C*s, *D*s, and *E*s you have, and then find your clutter communication type in the list below. It's possible to be a combination of two or more types.

IF YOU CHOSE MOSTLY *A*s: You're a *Talker*. When you're feeling cluttered, physically, mentally, or emotionally, you sit down and discuss it calmly and rationally. Congratulations! You already know what it takes many adults their entire lives to learn—that the best way to deal with any situation is to face it head-on in a straightforward yet balanced way. You don't bottle everything up, to later explode. And the people around you appreciate it. Just make sure that you don't end up using constant talking as a substitute for action. There is a time and place for discussion, but there's also a time and place for rolling up our sleeves and getting to work.

IF YOU CHOSE MOSTLY *B*s: You're a *Yeller*. Well, look at it this way—the good news is that you're not afraid to express your feelings! The bad news is that when you express your feelings, you do it VERY VERY LOUDLY. And, ironically, Yellers often have a hard time getting themselves heard. Why? Because as soon as most people hear yelling, they shut off. Their first thought is usually something along the lines of, *Why is this person yelling at me, and how can I get them to stop?* or, *Yelling! Oh! Time to yell back!* And neither of these reactions is going to get you heard and get you what you want. Communicating can be hard and, especially when dealing with clutter, really frustrating. Being surrounded by clutter (both inside and out) makes *everyone's* fuse shorter. But learning to modulate your tone is not only a skill that will help you when it comes to dealing with your clutter; it's a skill that will help you when dealing with your entire life. So take a deep breath, count to ten, picture a waterfall, or do whatever random thing helps you relax before bringing up difficult issues. You'll feel better, your loved ones will feel better, and you're much more likely to get what you want.

IF YOU CHOSE MOSTLY *C*s: You're a *Fumer*. When you were a little kid, your mom or your dad was probably really good at figuring out what you were thinking without you ever having to say anything. As a result you got used to feeling like everyone could read your mind. Then again, maybe, quite the opposite was true. Maybe you were constantly told to keep quiet whenever you expressed any feelings of dissatisfaction. And so you figure if you're upset, better to keep it to yourself than say anything about it and potentially rock the boat.

Well, whatever the reason behind it, somewhere along the way you got used to staying quiet when you had something to say. So now, when you're feeling overwhelmed by clutter, yours or others', emotional, physical, or mental, you stay quiet, hoping that someone will read your mind and help you. The problem is, you're older now, and you've gotten more complicated and probably a lot harder to read. And if no one happens to figure out what you're upset about, you sit there getting more and more upset, hoping someone will notice. And then feeling ignored, hurt, and pissed off when they don't.

In magic land everyone can read each other's minds. But here on regular earth, when we want or need something, we *have* to tell people if we want any chance of getting it. Feeling ignored and helpless is no fun at all, but it is *your* responsibility to make yourself heard. So next time you're feeling cluttered or overwhelmed, speak up!

IF YOU CHOSE MOSTLY *D*s: You're a *Doer*. The rarest of the bunch, Doers are constantly proactive about their clutter situations. Good for you! You take charge of your life and your clutter, and your reward is a more peaceful environment and a greater sense of control. That said, constantly taking care of *other* people's clutter, or never asking for help when you need it, is bound to take its toll eventually, not only on you but on your relationships, too. Sometimes we all need to talk, all of us. Especially when the clutter is mental or emotional.

IF YOU CHOSE MOSTLY *E*s: You're an *Avoider*. An Avoider, well, avoids situations like the clutter entirely. An Avoider will see a cluttered room and close her eyes and picture a less cluttered room and pretend that is the one she is in. An Avoider will feel overwhelmed with work and school and family life but will keep a smile on her face. Unlike Fumers, Avoiders aren't hiding their feelings. They're not necessarily even aware that they have the feelings in the first place! The problem is, when it comes to clutter, it *can't* be avoided. Avoiding clutter doesn't make it go away. It only makes it worse. Until you face the clutter in your life, you'll have no chance of getting rid of it. And it's only on the other side of clutter—when the clutter is not just shoved in a drawer, under a bed, or into the backs of our minds, but gone—that we can truly be happy.

CHAPTER SUMMARY . . .

Your clutter affects the people around you, and you are affected by theirs! But when it comes to communicating about your clutter, some ways are more helpful than others. Keeping calm, staying reasonable, and being proactive will help when clutter conflicts come up.

WHAT COMES NEXT . . .

Congratulations! You've made it this far. You've done a lot of the hard mental work necessary to prepare. Now it's time to get down to it and give your clutter the heave-ho!

What do Stephanie Scatterini, Devon DiSapoint, Jasmine Jumbleton, Sheila McShambles, Heather McHavoc, Caleb Clutterberg, José Hoardez, and Tessa and Jessa Messerton all have in common? They're all cluttered, and they could all use a serious decluttering, of course, but more than that—none of them has quite accepted the fact that their life is *their life.* If they want to be happy, every single one of them is going to have to imagine the life they want to live and set clear, uncluttered goals for themselves and their future.

IT'S YOUR LIFE. OWN IT!

This is your life.

It's not your parents' life, it's not your friends' life, it's not your teachers', it's not your siblings' or your cousins'. It's not the life of that guy over there or that girl over there. It's not the life of a TV character or someone in a movie or a character in a book.

For the vast majority of your life up until this point, your life wasn't really your own. But it's yours now. It's the most valuable thing you'll ever have. And okay, so you *still* have plenty of rules to follow, but even when you're an adult, there will be rules to follow. Now, for the first time, you're old enough to make your own choices. And these choices affect everything you do.

How does being organized fit into all of this? Well, when you're really organized, you're acting with intention—everything (and everyone) in your life is there for a reason, a reason that you're aware of. A reason that makes sense, that feels right, and that moves your life in the direction you choose.

When you're organized, you have a general plan for your life. This doesn't necessarily mean you have to have every last detail written out on a giant poster board, but it does mean that you've really thought about it, and you know the direction in which you want to be headed. You've imagined the life you want to live, and you're ready to take action to bring that life out of your imagination and into reality.

If the life you want to live includes being part of a large group of friends who spend weekend afternoons playing Frisbee at the park, you will not wait to meet a group of people who are already playing Frisbee at the park or wait for someone to invite you in. You will start your own group; you will organize and invite. And if you've always dreamed of being a singer in a band, you won't just think about it every night before you go to sleep and only live this in your dreams. You will find people who want to be in your band with you, and then you will begin to practice.

You don't just let things happen and hope that at some point the life you want will magically appear with you in the center of it. You know that if you don't do it for yourself, no one will. So take a deep breath and get ready to have the life you want. After you turn the next page, your life will not be the same. And you only have your clutter to lose and everything to gain. Ready?

Now let's go . . .

PART 2

A STEP-BY-STEP GUIDE TO DECLUTTERING YOUR SPACE

AND NOW IT'S TIME TO GET STARTED ON THE NITTY-GRITTY OF DECLUTTERING.

The good news is you've done some of the hard work already. You've thought about your internal clutter and where it comes from. You've thought about your external clutter: You took stock of what it is, how it affects you, and how you tend to treat it. You've reimagined the SWYKS, and you've confronted some of the hurdles that might have been holding you back. And you've asked yourself the most important question of all and begun to imagine the life you want to live. You've started to think about how your *stuff* will bring you toward or away from it.

Changing (or even starting to change) your relationship with your stuff requires a big brain shift. But by taking the quizzes and asking yourself the tough questions and really looking at your situation, chances are by now you've already begun the process.

What you're about to do next isn't just "cleaning." Other times when you've cleaned your room, it was just about taking the stuff you had and getting it to "look neat." However, this process isn't just about making things look pretty, but about purging the crap out of your life so there's more room for what's really important. This is *not* just about throwing things away (although you will be doing a lot of that!). Rather, this is about figuring out what you really use and really need and making sure these things have room to breathe.

In the pages that follow I'll walk you through four simple steps to take you from cluttered with crap to free and clear.

FROM CLUTTERED TO CLEAR, IN FOUR EASY(ISH) STEPS

1 KICK START.

This is a quick and dirty beginning to the decluttering process. Here's where we'll be getting rid of a lot of the crap you've accumulated. We won't be making any hard choices here; our goal will be to get rid of as much of the stuff as quickly as possible.

2 HASH IT OUT.

Here's where we figure out what belongs in the zones. Here's where we make an individual chart for each of your zones to figure out what items you actually need and want in your life.

3

CONQUER THE SWYKS.

Here's where we take your charts and put your plans into action. Here's where we do the final stage of the current decluttering.

4

KEEP IT UP!

Here's where we talk about some strategies to adopt for the future so that you'll never end up trapped under a snowdrift of clutter again.

CHAPTER 9

KICK START

The goal of the first step in the
decluttering process is to get as much random crap
out of your SWYKS as possible. We're not going to
make any tough decisions just yet. This isn't the
time to decide whether or not to keep that box of old
birthday cards, or what to do with that clay "dog"
you made in third grade (which, okay, let's be honest
here, looks a lot more like a turtle). This isn't the
time for stressing over how to organize everything.
This is not the time for engaging in intense thought
about *anything*. This is the time for one thing and
only one thing: getting rid of as much stuff as you
can, as quickly as possible.

Note: Once you begin the first step of the decluttering process, make a deal with yourself that you won't bring any new stuff into the SWYKS until you're done with your decluttering. I know, I know, this might sound difficult, if not impossible. Especially if many of your social interactions involve things like trips to the mall. But it's impossible to declutter if you keep getting more clutter before you even begin!

Lazy Clutter Versus Stored Treasure

Most clutter falls into one of two categories: Lazy Clutter or Stored Treasure. Lazy Clutter is the kind of random stuff that seems to migrate into everyone's life if they're not making a conscious effort to avoid it. Lazy Clutter is mostly random crap that accumulated in the SWYKS because you didn't think that much about it one way or the other. You bought a magazine, so you tossed it on your dresser; you got a free T-shirt, so you draped it over the back of your chair. It's the easiest type to get rid of, because we don't really care about this stuff. Stored Treasure, however, can be a little trickier to deal with. Stored Treasure includes things that you cannot imagine living without, even if you do not actually use or want these things. Later we'll discuss how to honor your Stored Treasure in the best way possible. But for now leave the Stored Treasure alone. The Kick Start is just about dealing with the Lazy Clutter and getting rid of it as quickly as possible.

ASSEMBLE YOUR SUPPLIES

For this part of the decluttering process you don't need very many supplies. All you need are garbage bags (the bigger the better) and recycling bags. You also might want to invest in three inexpensive tarps on which to place the items in the SWYKS once you've decided where they fall. The tarps should be labeled TKO (which I'll explain on the next page).

SET A TIME

After school? During the weekend? After your sports practice? Whatever time you pick, choose carefully, and then *stick to it*. Write it on your calendar; set an alarm in your cell phone. If something better comes along, tough cookies. Unless you're missing graduation or the prom, right now your decluttering is more important anyway.

PICK THE SWYKS

You can't do everything at once, so make sure the area you're decluttering is reasonable given the amount of time you have. You might decide to take a weekend and do all the SWYKS at once (leaving some time on Friday or Monday to declutter your locker at school). Or, if you can only do a single day of decluttering, you might want to declutter your entire bedroom, and then save your trunk, bathroom shelf, and locker for your next decluttering appointment. Regardless, make sure you leave yourself enough time to really get the job done. There's nothing worse than setting a day to declutter and ending up running out of time, putting everything back where it was, and wasting all your hard work.

KNOCK OUT YOUR CLUTTER WITH A TKO

Have you ever heard the term "TKO"? TKO is an acronym used in boxing, which stands for "Technical Knockout." This term is used when a fight is stopped because one fighter is likely to be more seriously hurt, or already is, or is simply unable to continue. But here in the land of decluttering "TKO" has a different meaning, and we use it when we are knocking out our clutter. "TKO" stands for "Trash, Keep, Out-the-Door." These are the names of the three categories we're dealing with when we're talking about the Kick Start. When we're attempting to get rid of your surface clutter, every single item we encounter, every single item you *own*, will be put into one of these three simple categories.

T—TRaSH

Now, I know you might be thinking, "But um, I'm not gross. I don't *have* any trash in my room!" Only, trust me, I assure you, you actually do. My clients are almost always surprised by how much actual trash they have in their homes taking up valuable space that could be used for something else. When I say trash, I'm not just talking about empty Soy Crisp bags and used tissues. Things that belong in the Trash category include everything from actual garbage to broken and crappy items that need to be tossed out or recycled, and things like junk mail and old magazines that you're hanging on to for really no reason. This category also includes things like flash cards you've made for tests you've already taken and flyers for events that have already happened. When it comes to this Kick Start decluttering, think of the trash pile as your very, very, very hungry friend. Your friend, in fact, is starving. Feed it some delicious trash or food for recycling!

K—Keep

The Keep pile should contain only stuff that you love and use all the time—things that contribute to your life in a significant way. These items are not just space-taker-uppers. The Keep pile also might include the few pieces of Stored Treasure that you don't know what to do with just yet. Keep in mind: The fewer things you put in this pile, the less work you'll have to do later.

O—OUT-THE-DOOR

These are items that have no place in your life, but that won't just be recycled or thrown away. Once an item is put in the Out-the-Door pile, it will not work its way back into your living space. Items that belong in the Out-the-Door pile include anything that does not belong in your life anymore but that you are certain (certain!) would be valuable to someone else. Don't convince yourself that people want your random crap just because you cannot bring yourself to call it trash. A stained, ripped, T-shirt that you got for free, emblazoned with the logo of an energy drink, is not going to be valuable to anyone; this is trash, not something for you to pass along. All items in the Out-the-Door category will either be sold or donated. Your pile of Out-the-Door items might include old electronics you don't use anymore, clothes you no longer wear, books you've read and do not plan to read again, or any of the following.

Anything that does not belong to you: Your space is your space. It should not be filled with random things other people don't have room for. Clutter is bad for you, whether you're consciously thinking about it or not. If your friend doesn't have room for five "backup outfits" in her own school locker, you can offer to help her get decluttered so that they'll fit, but do not offer to keep her stuff in yours. It might be hard to say no, especially if you technically have room, but remember, your space is for your stuff, not someone else's.

Anything that you haven't used in twelve months: (Although some of the items you haven't used in twelve months might just be trash.) If you haven't used it in twelve months, you don't need it to be part of your life. It's that simple. It can be hard to get rid of things you spent a lot of money on, especially if you were *certain* you were going to use them all the time when you bought them. But if you don't use something, you don't use it. And if you don't use it and it's in the SWYKS, it's clutter. Clutter robs us of happiness, creativity, and joy. Keeping something you don't use just because you once paid money for it is like staying at a movie you hate because you already paid for the ticket. Once the money is gone, the money is gone. Going forward all you can do is cut your losses and try to make your current situation the best it can be.

A FEW NOTES ABOUT SELLING YOUR STUFF

Don't keep items "to sell later" if you know you don't actually have the time to do this. I've seen way too many people put tons of items in the Out-the-Door pile only to find that six months later their entire pile is still sitting in the back of their closet or in their garage because no one had time to deal with all of it.

eBay versus Garage Sales

Before you decide to sell a particular item on eBay, look up how much money similar items are being sold for. And remember, your time is valuable. If you look on eBay and find out that the "collectible" mug you're getting rid of has been selling for only $1.25

at auction, it's probably a better use of your time to donate it and be done with it. That said, current electronics and other high-priced items are often worth trying to sell online. If you're trying to sell an old iPod or those video games you no longer play, eBay just might be the place to do it.

You also might want to consider Internet consignment stores for some of your more expensive stuff. There are companies who specialize in selling other people's things. They'll take a percentage of the profits but do all of the work. It's worth it!

Garage sales, however, can be the perfect way to sell a lot of items at once, especially the sorts of items people would want to see in person before buying, or things that it would be difficult or not worth it to ship. If you don't have enough Out-the-Door items to host an entire garage sale on your own, it can be fun to team up with family members, neighbors, and friends and have a garage sale as a group. This can be especially fun if you're all decluttering at the same time.

DeCLUTTeR BUDDY

And speaking of decluttering with a friend, as we get into the down and dirty part of this decluttering, it helps to recruit what I like to call a Declutter Buddy. A Declutter Buddy is someone who has decided to declutter his or her life at the same time you're decluttering yours. While it is certainly not necessary to have others there to declutter with you, it can certainly make the whole thing a lot more fun. The ideal Declutter Buddy is a friend or family member who is embarking on his or her own mission to declutter, so you can do some of these exercises together and help each other keep motivated and stay on track.

SONGS TO DeCLUTTeR BY

You know what makes everything better? Music! So before you begin, pick out a couple of CDs, or download some tunes you find inspiring, or make a playlist of fun, upbeat music. Stumped for what to include? Here are a few songs you might consider adding to your Songs to Declutter By playlist:

"TALLY HO!"
by the Clean

"HOUSEWORK"
by the B-52's

"SPRING CLEANING"
by Hot Pursuit

"I CAN SEE CLEARLY NOW"
by Johnny Nash

"CLEANING OUT MY CLOSET"
by Eminem

"A SPOONFUL OF SUGAR"
from Mary Poppins (what, it's catchy!)

"1234"
by Feist

The best songs to include on a decluttering mix are the types of songs that are so catchy you find it impossible not to sing along or dance to them. Dancing and singing are two things that you can totally do while you're decluttering, so if it makes the process more fun, then do it!

NOW THAT YOU'RE READY ... LET'S GO!

A few final suggestions:

START ON TIME. You can be fashionably late for a debutante ball, your prom, or a big dinner party. *Do not be fashionably late for your own decluttering.* This is an important day. Set a time and stick to it.

IMAGINE THE LIFE YOU WANT TO LIVE. Remember to keep the life you want to live fresh in your mind as you go. Whenever you're torn about whether to put an item in the Keep pile, instead of asking yourself a hundred complicated questions—Do I need seven bags of colored Popsicle sticks? Is it a good idea to save my old toothbrush? Where did this big shoe come from?—ask yourself one simple one: Does this item go along with the life I want to live? That's the only question you need to ask yourself. And if the answer is no, you know where that item needs to go!

Don't waste time. As you declutter, you'll probably end up finding a lot of stuff that you haven't seen in a very long time— pictures from your best friend's twelfth birthday, old notes

your buddy passed you in class, that book report you did on *Goodnight Moon* in first grade, maybe even some stuff you thought you lost. But now is not the time to take a leisurely stroll down memory lane. You can look at it all later; for now just touch an item once, decide which pile it goes in, and move on.

Make your piles. You can't "Keep" everything! Make sure that your piles are pretty even in size. If you're trying to put everything in the Keep pile, you're not really doing what you set out to do. This process is about getting rid of as much stuff as possible. For every item you keep, you should aim to put one item in the Trash pile and one item in the Out-the-Door pile.

Don't stop until you're done. The most discouraging thing you can do during a Kick Start is to stop in the middle and leave the SWYKS messier-looking than when you started. When you're done for the day, put all the Keep items back where you found them (we'll find more permanent places for them later). Bring the Trash out to the garbage and the recycling bin. And get the Out-the-Door stuff out the door! Load anything you're donating directly into the car so either you or a kind family member can bring it to the drop-off spot for a local charity. Find a place to keep any items you're planning on selling—a place where they'll be out of the way. But remember, don't just leave these items there. If more than a few weeks have passed since you decluttered and you still haven't sold these items, it's probably time to donate them to a worthy cause.

Evaluate and Congratulate. Once you finish the Kick Start for one of the SWYKS, repeat it in all the SWYKS until the first layer of clutter has been removed. Then look around. *Aaaaaah.* The SWYKS probably look somewhat better already. And if you'd accumulated a lot of surface crap, they might look a whole lot better. Great job! You've done a lot of work already, and you should certainly celebrate your success. In fact the SWYKS might look so much better that you'll be tempted to say this is "good enough" and that it's time to stop. But don't! We're not done yet!

CHAPTER 10

HASH IT OUT

As I said before, you've done
a lot of the hard work already—you've imagined the life
you want to live, and you've started to change the way
you think about the stuff in your life. You've gotten rid
of your surface layer of clutter, and now you're perfectly
ready to start making some really big differences in your
spaces and in your life. The next step is to figure out the
what, where, and why of all the stuff in your spaces.

WHAT DO YOU KEEP WHERE, AND WHY?

Look around your room at home; look in your locker
at school; look at your bathroom shelf. What do

you keep in each of these spaces, and why? You've probably thought about where your stuff goes to some extent—you keep some personal care products on your shelf in the bathroom; you keep some books in your locker; maybe you keep all your socks in the upper-right-hand drawer of your dresser, or you generally keep magazines on top of your nightstand. But did you ever really sit down and think about why you've picked the spot you've picked for each item? I'm going to guess no. Most people's stuff ends up where it ends up . . . for hardly any reason at all!

Maybe your mom used to put away your clean laundry, and she was the one who decided to keep all your socks in the upper-right-hand drawer of your

dresser. Or maybe one day you put a magazine on your nightstand and then decided to stack some other ones on top of it. Whatever the reason, chances are you never sat down and thought, *Where is the best place for me to keep my vintage toothbrush collection?*

Or, *Where should my favorite books go?* You just plopped those things down one day, and that's where they've been ever since. But now it's time to change all that. It's time to be conscious of where you put what and why. To begin, we're going to look at the SWYKS and think about how you'd like to use each one. We're going to do this by creating a Space Function Chart.

THE SPACE FUNCTION CHART

Sometimes without meaning to we can end up using a space for a purpose for which it was never intended. The trunk of your car becomes a makeshift closet; your locker at school becomes a storage space for the big discount package of deodorants that your dad bought at the bulk store. This can make you feel cluttered, disorganized, and out of control (not to mention embarrassed when your current crush opens your locker and sees the twenty-five sticks of Ultra Strength Smell Blocker).

Filling out a Space Function Chart can help determine what we really want from each particular space. We will look at what your space is being used for, and compare it to what you'd ideally like to use it for. Your chart should include each of the major SWYKS.

SAMPLE FILLED-IN SPACE FUNCTION CHART

BEDROOM	
WHAT DO YOU USE THIS SPACE FOR NOW?	Sleeping, homework, eating, relaxing, watching TV, making craft projects.
WHAT SHOULD THIS SPACE BE USED FOR?	Sleeping, homework, relaxing.
WHAT HAS TO GO:	Craft supplies, dirty dishes, the TV.

BATHROOM SHELF	
WHAT DO YOU USE THIS SPACE FOR NOW?	Face stuff that makes me break out, hair products I don't use, stuff I do use, my swim cap.
WHAT SHOULD THIS SPACE BE USED FOR?	Personal care products I actually use, my shower radio.
WHAT HAS TO GO:	Products I don't use, my swim cap.

BACKPACK	
WHaT DO you use THIS SPaCe FOR now?	Schoolbooks, sports equipment, old magazines, extra socks.
WHaT SHOULD THIS SPaCe Be useD FOR?	Schoolbooks, organizer, a snack.
WHaT HaS TO GO:	Sports equipment, old magazines, extra socks.

LOCKeR	
WHaT DO you use THIS SPaCe FOR now?	Extra clothes, school projects I forgot to bring home, old notebooks, three extra jackets that I left in there by accident.
WHaT SHOULD THIS SPaCe Be useD FOR?	Sports equipment, Band-Aids and a couple of "for emergency" items, a sweater.
WHaT HaS TO GO:	Old notebooks, extra jackets, old projects.

CaR	
WHAT DO YOU USE THIS SPACE FOR NOW?	Stuff I want to return but haven't gotten around to returning yet, some of my friends' clothes, a sleeping bag from when I went camping four months ago, ice scraper, spare tire, a bowling ball (who even knows why that's in there).
WHAT SHOULD THIS SPACE BE USED FOR?	Ice scraper, spare tire, jumper cables.
WHAT HAS TO GO:	Everything else that's in there now!

NOTE ABOUT SHARED SPACES

Chances are, some of the SWYKS contain other people's stuff too. And if you're sharing a space with someone else, it can be especially difficult to get everything in order. Especially when the different people using a space have different ideas about what the purpose of the space should be.

For example, if you share a car with your brother, he might think the trunk is the perfect place to keep a broken guitar that he is kind of one day planning to take to get fixed (maybe). Or you might think that the living room is the ideal place for you to keep all your craft supplies, but your parents or siblings might disagree with you.

When figuring out the ideal function of each of the SWYKS, you should definitely pay special attention to the spaces you share with others. So many conflicts are the result of people simply having a different idea of what their spaces should be used for. Instead of assuming that you and the other members of your family (or your friends) agree on the ideal purpose of your shared spaces, you should sit down and discuss it. Reading it like this seems obvious, but so often people just assume they have the same idea and never talk about it!

zones

Unless you live in a mansion or a castle, it's likely that all the SWYKS are serving multiple purposes. Your bedroom is where you sleep, relax, and do homework, and maybe it's where you use the Internet. Your backpack holds your books for school, but it also might hold other things you need—your cell phone, for example, or an iPod. So when trying to get organized, it can be very helpful to divide the SWYKS into zones.

What's a zone? A zone is a section of your space that contains one single type of item or items used for one single purpose or activity. Dividing your spaces into zones helps you figure out how much space you have for those things and where particular items should go, and helps you better judge if these items are out of order.

Have you ever been to a Japanese restaurant and ordered lunch or dinner in a bento box? A bento box is a special kind of box in which food is served. But unlike the plates that the majority of Americans use at their dinner tables, a bento box is divided up into a number of different sections. If you order a bento box at a Japanese restaurant, you might find that one section of the box contains a California roll. And another section might contain some chicken teriyaki. In another section you'll find some rice. Another might hold a couple of dumplings. The rice and the dumplings aren't mixed together. And the chicken teriyaki and the California roll aren't in the same compartment. Every item or type of item has its own place, separate from the other items. So, going forward, let's imagine all the SWYKS are big bento boxes. Each little compartment is a zone. When thinking about what zones belong in each room, the main questions you need to ask yourself are: What is this space for? How much room do I have? Are the items in a zone all of the same type?

BEDROOM

Sleeping
Relaxation
Homework
Clothes I wear
Shoes
Off-season clothes
Books
Music
Photos

BATHROOM SHELF

Face soap
Zit stuff
Body lotion

BACKPACK

Notebooks for school
Clothes
Makeup
Wallet

HASH IT OUT

183

LOCKER

Books
Extra school supplies
After-school sports
    equipment
Emergency items
    (Band-Aids, safety
    pins, first-aid kit)
Supplies for art class

CAR

Emergency items
    (jumper cables,
    spare tire)
Stuff to bring to
    babysitting
Registration and
    insurance papers
Maps

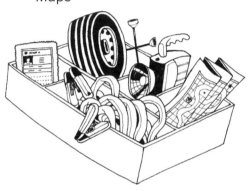

GIVING EACH ZONE A HOME

But it's not just about figuring out what makes up each zone; it's about figuring out where each zone should be situated. Which means we have to make choices. For example: You need a space for your books, do you want that to be in your desk drawer or on your bookshelf? Would out-of-season clothes be better stored in the back of your closet or in that trunk at the foot of your bed? Would you rather sleep in your bed or on your bookshelf?

Okay, kidding about the last one. Certain zones will have obvious homes. But don't be afraid to get creative and set things up according to your personal needs and preferences. For example, if you have a big closet that holds all your clothes and a giant, mostly empty dresser, there's no reason not to fill it up with the books you love that have no other set spot.

THE STRAGGLERS

As you are figuring out your zones, you'll inevitably find that there are some extra items that are just hanging around even though there is really no place for them to go. These stray bits of clutter are wandering aimlessly around your room looking for a space to set up camp: a single shoe (its mate mysteriously disappeared last year), that free beach ball you won in a raffle that you've never even blown up (but couldn't bear to part with during the Kick Start). Where should these things make their home? ANYWHERE BUT IN THE SWYKS! If something is straggling around in your room, you need to ask yourself why. If it doesn't belong in any of your zones, and it's not a piece of stored treasure that you can't bear to part with right now (we'll discuss that more on pages 198–199), chances are it's clutter and you don't need it.

Now that we've hashed it out, it's time to make it real. . . .

CHAPTER 11

CONQUER THE SWYKS

Now it's time to take your space
Function Chart, keep in mind the vision for the life you want to live, and begin to make your spaces as beautiful, functional, and organized as can be. Even though you've done lots of preparation and Kick Started your decluttering, I understand that this stage of the process can still seem kind of overwhelming. But don't panic! It took you a long time to get to your current state of clutter, and you should expect that it's going to take a while to get rid of it all. But no matter how big a project it is, you should begin to tackle it the way you'd start any project of any size. Don't expect to jump right in and do the entire thing

in fifteen minutes—you need to divide it into little steps and do one at a time.

FOR EACH OF YOUR SPACES, TAKE THE FOLLOWING THREE STEPS:

1 THINK IT THROUGH: **This means looking realistically at the space, thinking about where most of the clutter comes from, thinking about the biggest problem areas, and considering what doesn't belong.**

2 SET IT UP: **This involves looking at your Space Function Chart and vowing to keep nothing in your spaces that doesn't serve a purpose in your life.**

3 GET IT DONE: **I think we all know what this means.**

If you're too overwhelmed to do everything at once, you can divide your decluttering into half-hour segments. Make a thirty-minute decluttering playlist, or set the alarm on your cell phone for a half hour from when you start.

And then that's it—just get going!

Don't worry about the future or the past; don't worry about how you're going to get it all done. Your only concern should be doing the best you can in the next half hour.

Okay, maybe some of what I'm about to suggest here you already took care of during the Kick Start. So if any of this is old news, well then good for you. You've really been sticking to the plan! But if any of this is new, well then now is the time to really get down to it.

BEDROOM

For most of you reading this book, your bedroom isn't just the place you sleep; it's the place you *live.* For adults who own an entire house, a bedroom is just a bedroom. For teens, however, a bedroom can easily end up functioning more like a studio apartment. Maybe you do your homework in your bedroom. Use the Internet. Talk on the phone. Read books or magazines. Hang out with your friends. Your bedroom probably needs to fill many functions in your life, and that's all the more reason that it needs to be clutter-free. To begin, we'll tackle your zones one at a time:

CLOTHES

Most people in this country have way more clothes than they actually wear. Tastes change. Seasons change. Styles change. You grow an inch. You gain a few pounds. If you find your closet overrun with things you're not wearing, you are not alone. But now is the time to let a lot of that stuff go.

YOU SHOULD ONLY KEEP CLOTHING ITEMS THAT:

1 LOOK GREAT ON YOU. There are enough different styles of clothing out there that there is no reason to wear anything that doesn't flatter you. Everyone is different, and everyone looks best in different styles or colors. A really expensive sweater in a color that happens to make you look like you have the flu is no more valuable to you than an ugly sweater that's full of holes. People look good in different things, and just because your best friend looks great in mustard yellow doesn't mean you're going to. And that's okay! If it doesn't look great on you, it doesn't matter how "nice" it is—it's not for you!

2 MAKE YOU FEEL GREAT. You know how there are some outfits that make you feel fantastic every time you put them on? Maybe it's your favorite pair of perfectly worn jeans, or maybe it's that secondhand leather jacket that makes you feel like a rock star. Or maybe it's just a white T-shirt that's as soft as a blanket and fits just right. Whatever it is, *all* your clothes should make you feel this great, or close to. If there's a certain shirt that always makes you feel like you're a lumpy sack of potatoes, or a pair of jeans that always ride up, *get rid of them*. Life's too short to be uncomfortable when you don't have to be.

③ FIT YOU *NOW.* You grew two inches last summer, and ever since then your favorite dress is way too short. Or that T-shirt you used to love fits you like a sausage casing. Or maybe those jeans you used to love cannot be zipped up anymore if you, y'know, intend to breathe. Bodies change, and the same clothes don't last forever. If something doesn't fit you now, right now, do not keep it.

AND DEFINITELY GET RID OF:

① CLOTHING YOU NEVER WEAR. Remember that pair of engineer pants that looked so great in the store but that you hated as soon as the tags were removed? And that shirt that looks cool but feels like it's made of sandpaper? If you haven't worn something in twelve months because it's never seemed like the right time, it probably never will be. Get rid of it, cut your losses, and give yourself back the space it's taking up.

② CLOTHES THAT ARE STAINED, RIPPED, OR FALLING APART. Okay, we're not talking about things that are intentionally ripped or intentionally stained; we're talking about clothes that have encountered terrible and tragic fates: your favorite dress, which was the victim of a ketchup collision, or those dress pants, which were so nice . . . until they got caught on a nail. You imagine that *one day* you'll try that stain-removing secret you read about on the Internet, or that you'll sit down at the sewing machine and magically know how to use a sewing machine and then fix those pants. But if that *one day* isn't going to be anytime in the next two weeks, then *get rid of it.*

If you're not entirely sure what you have and haven't worn in the last twelve months, try this: Turn all the hangers in your closet so that the hooks on the hangers are facing the back of the closet. Every time you wear something, put it back in the closet with the hook facing *front.* At the end of twelve months all the items that are still facing the back will be clothes you haven't worn. Which means it's time for them to go! By the way—if you're really brave, you might want to try this for six months. Either way, I promise you'll be surprised by the outcome.

SMOOTH FABRIC + SMOOTH PLASTIC OR METAL HANGERS + GRAVITY = A CLOSET THAT'S A BIG MESS.

Is the floor of your closet a big old mess of clothes that gravity has yanked off their hangers? And have you stopped bothering to rehang them because you know they're just going to fall again? Then do yourself a favor and invest in some hangers that will keep your poor clothes from succumbing to gravity's clutches. Any regular home-goods store has an entire hanger department *filled* with dozens of different kinds of hangers. Mixed in are some that are covered in a fuzzy flocking material. These hangers provide more friction and keep your clothing from sliding off. Hang a clothing item on one of these suckers just once, and it's there to stay until it's time to wear.

SHOES

People tend to get awfully attached to their shoes, more so than to other items of clothing in their closet. This makes sense—not only are shoes expensive, but people often use their footwear to define their personal styles. A pair of baby-blue boots can turn a regular outfit into something special. And metallic silver sandals can make the simplest black dress into a fancy-occasion-worthy ensemble. But just because shoes can make an outfit doesn't mean you have to keep every pair you've ever owned *forever*. If your sneakers are worn out and you got a new pair, there's no reason to hang on to the old ones. You don't need more than a few pairs of flip-flops. Take old boots to get reheeled or get rid of them. If you have a pair of shoes that hurt, and every time you wear them for an hour you think your pinky toe is going to fall off, bring them to a shoe repair person and see about getting them stretched. And if they're

still not comfortable?
Get rid of them. It can
seem like a waste to
wear a really cool pair of
shoes only one time, but
if they hurt, they hurt.

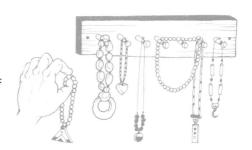

JeWeLRY/ACCessoRies

Jewelry and other accessories don't take up much
space, but they can be awfully hard to store.
Necklaces get knotted. Earrings get lost behind the
dresser. And all those little boxes they come in take
up space. So get rid of the boxes and instead find a
system for storing everything together so it looks neat
and organized. Get creative! A wall-mounted tie rack
makes a great place to hang long necklaces. A bamboo
place mat affixed to the wall (so that the slats are
parallel to the floor) makes a cool-looking earring rack.

Trendy costume jewelry can be relatively inexpensive,
but it doesn't always last long. Gold-colored earrings
eventually turn silver. Rhinestones fall out of
bracelets. If a piece of jewelry is broken and too
inexpensive to be worth fixing, get rid of it! The same
goes for jewelry you never wear. If you haven't worn it
in a year, you're probably never going to.

BOOKS

I love books and I love reading, but just because
you've read and enjoyed a book doesn't mean you
have to have it on your shelf until the end of time.
Being a book lover and a well-read person is not the
same thing as *owning* a lot of books. Some people
own dozens if not hundreds of books they've never
read, and some people have read hundreds of books
and own very few. Don't mistake the paper and the
cover that make up the book for the knowledge
inside of it or the experience of having read it. Once
you've read a particular book, *you've read that book*,
and whether or not you have that book on your shelf
is irrelevant.

If you have space on your shelves for books you've
never read or will never read again, then by all means
keep them! Having a large book collection can be a
source of pride, but books do take up an awful lot
of space, and if you only have room for a certain
fraction of your book collection, then you might
want to consider getting rid of those books that were
simply entertaining and not life-enriching in some
way. Only keep books that mean something to you.
That book you got at the airport for seven dollars and
abandoned halfway through your flight in favor of the
in-flight magazine doesn't count. Hang on to books

that mean something to you personally, and if your decluttering requires it, it is okay to let the rest go.

There are plenty of places to donate books you don't have space for—hospitals, shelters, and even libraries are usually quite happy to have the extra books. Or think about arranging a book swap program with a few of your friends. You'll reduce your clutter and save money, too.

DESK

What do you do at your desk? Do you do homework? Study for tests? Check Facebook? Write e-mails? IM your friends? Great, so then what's with the mini Slinky and all those *Family Guy* bobbleheads? Desks can get overrun with "fun" toys that aren't really that much fun and only serve as a cluttery distraction. When you're trying to work, a clean desk area is your best buddy. Keep random toys somewhere else. The surface of a well-organized desk should be mostly empty, but don't let all that tempting clear space be an invitation for clutter to jump up on it and party down! You'll get more work done in a clutter-free environment.

What else is causing your desk clutter? Homework assignments? Notes for projects you're working on? Tests you've finished but will need to review for the final exam at the end of the year? Great. But having all this stuff mixed together is confusing and makes it hard to find what you need when you need it. When trying to organize a messy pile of papers, remember that it always helps to keep like items together.

Get a wire basket and make this your "in-box." Your in-box will hold any items that need to be dealt with immediately—homework assignments that need to be completed, permission slips that need to be filled out, job applications, etc.

Anything that doesn't need to be dealt with immediately should be off your desk, neatly stored away either in an inexpensive filing cabinet or accordion folder.

OLD SCHOOL SUPPLIES. Why do we all have so many pens? Is it because they're cheap? Easily lost? Who can say! All I know is that every house I've helped organize has, among the clutter, a number of extra pens. I've gone into houses that had *entire drawers* full of new, half-used, and dried-up pens and pencils. Pen manufacturers have made some stunning improvements in pen technology. Good for them. We have sparkly pens and pens with little toys on top balanced on springs, doctor-recommended pens and pens that write in space; there are even pens that play songs from *High School Musical*. Enough with all the crazy pens, people! Having a pen that smells like cinnamon or looks like a fish probably isn't going to make homework any more fun, even if we can briefly convince ourselves of that when we're at the store.

So get a pen you like that is comfortable to write with. Get a backup pen. And a couple of pencils. That's it. Throw out the extra pens and vow to never buy a pen again unless you actually need it!

Same goes for the rest of your extra school supplies. It's temping to get "a new one" of every item we have at the beginning of every year. We somehow trick ourselves into thinking that new products are going to make us more organized people. But *products* don't make us organized. We make ourselves organized, and the products are just tools that help.

STORED TREASURES

So the summers you spent at Camp Willowbrook may have been the source of some of your fondest memories and where you met some of your best friends. That's wonderful, but that doesn't mean you need to save your old, stained, worn, too-small Camp Willowbrook T-shirt until the end of time. There are ways to honor the past without taking up a lot of space. And rolling the shirt into a ball and sticking it in the back of your dresser is not what I'm talking about here.

If something is important enough to you to be worth saving, then it should be out and on display where you'll actually enjoy it. Instead of storing that old camp shirt in a drawer, cut off your camp logo and put it in a frame along with a picture of you and your camp friends. And then hang this picture up on your wall.

You can do the same for any other items that feel important to you and remind you of the past. But keep in mind, just because we tend to associate things we own with things that happen doesn't change the fact that the *object* is not the *experience*.

THE BED

Your bed is the most important part of your room. In fact your bedroom is named after it! So it should be a cozy, relaxing place to rest for the night (and have that recurring dream where you accidentally show up at school in your Halloween costume and a football helmet), *not* a storage area. Okay, so it's flat, and it's probably at a height that makes it convenient to toss stuff on it when you've just entered your room. But getting into the habit of keeping crap off your bed is a good idea. Your bed should hold sheets, pillows, blankets, and sometimes you. And that's it!

Oh, and I'm not trying to sound like your parents here, but seriously, come on, make your bed! An unmade bed is a sad and messy sight. If you're not going to make your hospital corners every morning, at the very least flap your comforter out on top of your bed. It takes less than ten seconds to do and makes your room look much neater.

And speaking of improving your room's looks—are you still using the same choo-choo train sheets you got when you were six? Because if so, it might be time to get a new set. Imagine the life you want to live. Does sleeping on top of a bunch of miniature trains fit into that life?

UNDER THE BED

Okay, so I may not be an astronomer, but I'm preeeeetty certain there's not a black hole under your bed. And as such, *putting stuff under there doesn't make it not exist anymore!* Yet, for some reason so many of us treat our under-bed areas as magical no-man's-lands in which things do not count. But hidden clutter is still clutter! In general, stuff people store under their bed is stuff they forget about. Unless you have a captain's bed or have a very small bedroom and a really great under-bed storage system that is actually convenient to use, your bed shouldn't be on top of anything except a bed frame, air, and the floor.

BaTHROOM SHELF

It seems that every time I walk into the pharmacy, a dozen brand-new personal care items have magically appeared on the shelves promising even *softer* skin, even *fewer* pimples, teeth so white you have to warn people not to look directly at them or they will risk blindness, breath so delicious that when you open your mouth strangers run toward you to get a whiff, *negative* body hair, and hair that smells so delightful people will think you've just been showering in a waterfall with a unicorn. The unfortunate reality is that most of these products are just slightly retooled versions of what was on the shelves the week before. But if you're like so many of us, you always have hope that *this* product is going to be the one that changes your life. And when it doesn't, you stick it up on your bathroom shelf and forget about it until you buy something new. Since something new comes out every week, it's no wonder that most of our bathroom shelves are a veritable orphanage of abandoned toiletries.

So why don't we get rid of these things? Is it because we're hoping at some point the shampoo that actually made us smell like we'd been showering with a *horse* will somehow start to smell good to us? If you bought a product and tried it out and simply didn't like it, many pharmacies will still be willing to take it back and offer you a full refund. Even if you've already used it! But it's probably too late for most of the stuff on your shelf now. If you have a bunch of nonexpired, barely used products, consider arranging a swap day with some of your friends. And if no one wants what you have? Toss it out!

As you're going through your bathroom shelf, make sure you check the expiration date on all your items. Makeup can go bad quickly, especially mascara, which is only good for two or three months; after that, bacteria builds up inside, and then you're just smearing bacteria near your eye. Gross!

BackPack

When you're decluttering your backpack, the first step is to dump everything out so you can sort through all the stuff. If your family home has carpeting, you might want to dump it on one of those tarps you bought during the Kick Start. If you don't have one, a ripped-open paper bag or shopping bag will do. And if your pack is really big? You might want to use a big trash bag. Remember what you did when you were doing the Kick Start? Now do it for your backpack. The first order of business is to divide everything into the TKO piles: Trash, Keep, Out-of-My-Bag!

And don't forget to check all of those extra pockets! If you have one of those backpacks with eight hundred different compartments, you might find that your bag is filled with duplicate items—replacements for items you thought you lost that were in fact just hiding in your third cell phone pocket.

Pay attention to what kind of stuff you're putting in the T and the O piles. If what you're getting rid of is mostly stuff you were too lazy to throw in the garbage—granola bar wrappers, gum wrappers, receipts you're not saving for any particular reason— make a vow here and now to get into the habit of throwing garbage away directly instead of putting it in your backpack and waiting to throw it away later. Does the life you want to live involve carrying a bunch of trash on your back all day? I didn't think so! Also, keep an eye out for items that work their way into your school bag even though they really don't need to be in there. For example, do you really need to be lugging *three* lip balms around with you all day? Couldn't you leave one on the bathroom shelf and put one of them on your nightstand? And what about that beret you brought with you to school when you were doing a presentation in French class? Do you *really* need to bring that to school with you every day?

Okay, so you've gotten rid of the trash, and you've taken all the Out-of-My-Bag stuff out of your bag. The remaining items are all things you want to keep in your bag, so you should dump everything back in, zip your bag up, and call it a day, right?

Well, by now you probably know what I'm going to say. . . .

As you put the items back in your bag, make sure you're really being vigilant about designating a home for each item. If you're one of those people who constantly thinks she's lost her cell phone or her keys because your bag has so many pockets, assigning each item to a particular part of your bag will probably save you a lot of time and aggravation. And if you know there are going to be short periods of time when you absolutely *must* keep some trash in your bag (say, gum wrappers while you're in class, etc), then designate one pocket as the "trash pocket," and make sure you empty it at least once a day.

SCHOOL LOCKER

School lockers contain
a very particular type
of clutter, which I like
to call Rushed Clutter!
You're probably only
at your locker when
you're in a hurry, and
if you're rushing to
class, you might not
have time to make sure

you're placing items neatly on the
hook or the shelf. But if you're mostly at your locker
when you're stressed or in a hurry, that's all the more
reason to make it organized and clutter-free.

Think of your locker as your teeny-tiny at-school
bedroom (well, except you don't actually go in it . . .
hopefully). A clutter-free locker will help make you
feel more focused and less stressed.

Chances are you don't have time to clean out your
locker during the school day, and if you're keeping a
lot of private stuff inside your locker, you might not
want to clean it out when that hot guy/girl from World
History could walk by at any moment. So instead
arrange a locker-cleaning date with your Declutter
Buddy one day after school. One of you brings the

trash bags; the other one brings an after-school snack. And then keep each other company while you get rid of the crap!

First, take everything out and do a Kick Start. Then consider what you're putting in the Trash and Out-of-My-Locker piles. If a lot of it is stuff you meant to take home days ago, you might want to invest in a magnetic or sticky-backed bin that you can stick to the side of your locker. Or designate one half of your locker as the "take home" side. Every time you put something in your locker that you mean to take home with you at the end of the day, put it in the designated area. Then when you're rushing out of school at the end of the day, you'll be less likely to forget something you meant to take with you.

CaR

Is your car a garbage bin on wheels? Do you keep half your closet in your trunk? Is your glove compartment a graveyard for broken CDs and expired batteries? Car clutter can be easy to ignore, since it's not even inside your house! And since most of the time we're in the car, the car is *moving*, it's probably not usually a good time to get out and throw that broken CD in the trash. But not only does a cluttered car make for an unsafe driving environment, but it makes for a not-so-much fun ride for your passengers.

Start off with a car Kick Start. Set three tarps or garbage bags out on your driveway, and take everything out of your front seat, backseat, trunk, cup holders, and glove compartment, and off the dashboard and place it on one of the tarps. Even if you didn't think your car was particularly cluttered, you might be surprised by how much *stuff* you've been driving around with. Now put everything into either the Trash, Keep, or Out-of-My-Car pile. (If you're finding that you have a huge trash pile, you should consider doing a trash check every time you get out of your car at the end of the day or, like I do, every time you fill the tank at the gas station.)

Then look at what's left. Sports equipment? Half of your best friend's wardrobe? Wherever most of your car clutter is coming from, now is the time to figure out a solution.

Before you put the Keep items back in the car, designate a particular storage area for each type of item and remember to keep all like items together. For example: Maybe you'll decide to keep your soccer cleats and shin guards in a bin on the right side of your trunk and your music stand and sheet music folder on the left. Make a habit of always putting the same type of item in the same place, and you'll have a less cluttered car and a much easier time finding things when you need them.

MISCELLaneOUS SPaCes

Okay, most likely there are Spaces Where You Keep Stuff that I haven't mentioned so far. But just because something isn't on this list doesn't mean you should ignore it! To put it another way, this list is only the beginning. The skills you've learned so far can be applied to both the zones I've discussed and any zones that are particular to you.

After you've finished decluttering all your personal spaces, it's time to go through your *entire house* room by room and look for anything else that's yours. Collect everything and take inventory. Does any of this stuff actually belong somewhere else? Is all of your stuff stored neatly? If your own DVDs are mixed in with your family's DVD collection, are all of them in the correct cases? Is any of this stuff actually trash? Is your stuff getting in the way of anyone else's? (Note: These are just a few examples of the types of clutter I've seen leaking out of teens' rooms and into the rest of the house. Just because I don't mention something here doesn't mean it might not count as clutter!) Going through your house and getting your own clutter out of the way is a great way to bring up the topic of decluttering with your entire household. (More on that later.)

But first . . .

HOORAY FOR YOU!!!!!

You've done the hard work of decluttering, and now it's time to celebrate!

After you've successfully gone clutter-free—and given yourself a few days or weeks to let it all sink in—you might want to take a few moments to sit down and think about all the ways in which your life has improved since you did it. Do you feel more focused and less stressed? Do you sleep better? Does your homework seem easier? Do you have more energy? Are you less irritated at your family? Having more fun with your friends? Just as living with clutter can affect every area of our lives, decluttering can affect every area of our lives too!

On the following pages, write down some ways in which you feel different since decluttering. Then later, if clutter begins to creep back in, you can remind yourself just how good it feels to be clutter-free.

WAYS IN WHICH THINGS ARE DIFFERENT SINCE I DECLUTTERED!

1 ....
....
....

2 ....
....
....

3 ....
....
....

4 ....
....
....

5 ....
....
....

6
....
....
....

7
....
....
....

8
....
....
....

9
....
....
....

10
....
....
....

CHAPTER 12

KEEP IT UP!

You've done a fantastic job so far—
you've changed your relationship with your stuff, you've made some tough decisions, you've done a Kick Start, and you've delved deeper into every nook and cranny of your clutter. But decluttering isn't just a one-time thing; you've got to keep it up! Or you'll very quickly find yourself dealing with . . .

CLUTTER . . . THE RETURN!

You spend all this time decluttering, and everything looks so great, but then you turn your back for a second and CLUTTER CREEPS BACK IN. How does

this happen? Well, quite easily, really, unless we're vigilant about it. You can't just expect to get rid of your clutter one time and then forget about it forever. Decluttering needs to become part of your daily routine. You need to take charge of your clutter each and every day.

Now, I know *every day* might sound like an awfully big commitment, but think about all the other things you do every day: You wake up, you brush your teeth, you take a shower, you get dressed, you eat breakfast, you go to school, you eat lunch, you eat dinner, you do your homework. Okay, so maybe you don't *love* doing *all* these things, but you probably don't have to think much about them either. You don't think. You just do.

Why?

Because you've made them into habits. And once you make something a habit, doing it every day doesn't seem like such a big deal.

DIRTY CLOTHES

When a recently decluttered room starts parading its way back into mess, dirty clothes are usually at the front of that parade, leading the way. As soon as dirty clothes start collecting around the room, it's easy to let all your other decluttering and cleaning efforts slide. The fix? Make sure you have a hamper, and make sure you actually use it!

If you plan to wear a particular item of clothing more than one time before you wash it, put it back in your closet or dresser; don't just leave it sitting on your desk or your chair. Clothes that will be worn again before they're washed should be put away, and clothes that are ready to be washed should go into the hamper. It's really not that complicated!

THE TEN-MINUTE RULE

If you devote just ten minutes every day to maintaining your clutter-free state, I can guarantee that you won't have to do another large-scale decluttering for an awfully long time. You'll be surprised at how much you can get done in ten minutes.

Five of these minutes should be for straightening up—putting books back on your bookshelf, throwing away any little bits of trash, making your bed, etc. And the other five minutes should be for getting rid of clutter. But wait, didn't you already get rid of all of your clutter? Yes, it's true. But yesterday's must-keep item isn't necessarily going to stay a must-keep item forever. You already got rid of most of your clutter in steps 2 and 3, but now that you've changed your relationship with your stuff, you might find yourself consistently finding you don't actually need items you thought you couldn't live without. So just because something made it through the first and second rounds of decluttering doesn't mean it'll necessary pass the daily clutter-kill.

Five minutes of cleaning, five minutes of decluttering. It's a small investment, but it's worth it.

I promise—that's really all it takes.

If at all possible, try scheduling your ten minutes at the same time every day. That will further help you turn your daily decluttering into a habit. Or if you want, divide your ten minutes into five-minute segments. Then do one segment every morning when you wake up and the other every night before you go to bed. And that's it!

THE IN/OUT RULE

This is one of the most important rules when it comes to clutter maintenance: For every new item you bring into your SWYKS, vow that you'll get rid of a similar item. If you buy a new shirt, donate an old shirt to a charity you like. If you get a new CD, find one you don't listen to anymore and give it away to a friend. In this way you'll never increase the overall amount of stuff you have, and you won't end up finding yourself with a ton of new things and nowhere to put them.

GIFT GIVING

All special occasions don't need to come with stuff attached. As we already discussed, we can make our friends and family feel special and loved on their birthdays without bogging them down with a bunch of stuff they don't want or need.

For example:

INSTEAD OF: giving your friend a CD . . .

WHY NOT: take her to see a concert.

INSTEAD OF: buying your friend an adventure movie on DVD . . .

WHY NOT: take him on an adventure in a neighboring town for the day.

INSTEAD OF: buying your friend some makeup . . .

WHY NOT: treat both of you to a pedicure at a spa.

INSTEAD OF: giving your friend a cookbook (you know he'll never use it) . . .

WHY NOT: sign the two of you up for a one-day cooking class.

INSTEAD OF: giving your friend a monkey T-shirt . . .

WHY NOT: take her to the monkey house at the zoo.

INSTEAD OF: buying your friend some random "stuff" just so you get credit for having given him a gift . . .

WHY NOT: offer to help him declutter!

Yes, there are some occasions for which giving a gift of a material item is expected, but on those occasions make sure you're giving your friend or family member something they'll really love. And if you're not sure, give them a gift certificate!

THREE THINGS TO DO BEFORE YOU BUY SOMETHING NEW

❶ WAIT forty-eight hours before you buy it.

❷ CALL your Declutter Buddy and run it by him/her.

❸ THINK about how much space this new "must have" item is going to take up. Can you think of where it will go in your room or locker? Is there space for it?

THE "I DIDN'T BUY IT" FUND

Every time you're about to buy something and don't, put the money you would have spent in a special "I didn't buy it" fund. Think of something really special that you'd like to do—a trip you'd like to take, or a special restaurant you'd like to eat at, or a play you'd like to see. At the end of a year you'll have enough money to have a really memorable experience that you'll remember long after you would have thrown away whatever it is you didn't buy.

PART 3

APPLYING THESE SKILLS TO THE REST OF YOUR LIFE

CHAPTER 13

YOUR EVERYDAY LIFE

The skills you've learned and the exercises you've done while reading this book don't just help when it comes to decluttering; they can help you with the rest of your life! Your everyday life, your school life, your family life, and your future life can all be improved if you start from a base of imagining the life you want to live and then take it from there. And remember, the term clutter doesn't just apply to physical clutter, but to emotional and mental clutter too. If you look at your entire life through the lens of the expert declutterer that you've now become, you'll see that a lot of the problems that keep you from living the life you'd like to be living come from one kind of clutter or another.

STARTING AND MANAGING YOUR DAY

I'll be the first to admit it: High school in this country starts
way too early. But even if you're not naturally a morning
person, there are plenty of things you can do to make starting
your day a whole lot easier.

1. IMAGINE THE DAY YOU WANT TO HAVE. Okay,
this is actually something to do the night *before* the morning.
It's a smaller version of imagining the life you want to live.
Don't think about the big picture; think about the little picture.
Imagine the day you want to have tomorrow. Think about
everything you have planned for the next day and imagine
how you'd like it to go. Pay special attention to anything you
might be nervous about—a math test, an audition for the
school play. Imagine getting an A-plus on your test, having
a great audition for your play, and so on. Don't spend your
time worrying about failure. Energy spent worrying is wasted
energy. Visualize everything going exactly how you'd like it to
go. (I don't, of course, mean to imply that visualization is all
you have to do to make your day go well. Although it should
be obvious, I'll just mention that in addition to visualizing a
perfect outcome, if you have a test, study, and if you have an

audition, practice! But beyond that, visualization can help too.) Going to sleep with positive thoughts in your head will make you sleep better, and if you make it a regular habit, you'll find yourself consistently waking up in a better mood.

② LEAVE YOURSELF AS LITTLE TO DO AS POSSIBLE IN THE MORNING. Put your homework in your bag before you go to sleep; pick out what you're planning on wearing the next day. You might not feel like doing these things at night, but you'll probably feel even less like doing them when you first wake up. If you can streamline what you need to do in the morning, you'll be able to start your day in a much calmer frame of mind.

③ START EVERY DAY WITH FIVE MINUTES OF FUN. I know you're rushed in the morning (although if you follow step 2, you might be slightly less rushed). No matter how rushed you are, vow to devote five minutes every morning to doing something fun. Dance to your favorite song, or spend five minutes reading a book or working on a non-school-related project or watching five minutes of your favorite comedian's DVD, or just spend five minutes laughing. Or meditating! (Just make sure you don't fall back to sleep.)

④ EAT BREAKFAST. Okay, I know, I know, I am obviously not the first person to tell you that breakfast is a good idea. Parents, teachers, magazine writers, newspaper editors, and the advertisers who make breakfast products all seem keen on telling you that you need a healthy breakfast to start your day. I'll join that list of people telling you that. Eat breakfast! If you don't have time in the morning, or if the idea of eating early in the day makes you want to barf, at the very least have a banana and a string cheese just so you're not going to school on an empty stomach. Having breakfast in the morning will put you in a better mood and make you more awake. It's that simple.

YOUR HEADSPACE

Just as it's impossible to focus on working toward having the life you want to live when your rooms, backpacks, and lockers are overrun with physical clutter, it's impossible to focus on having the life we want to live when your head is filled with mental clutter!

As we've already discussed, the first step to decluttering your mind is decluttering your spaces. And if you've been following along with this book so far, you've already done it! But that *alone* won't do it. We live in a society in which each and every one of us is receiving a constant influx of information:

Magazines tell us to be skinnier and to buy new clothes, advertisers tell us we need to have whiter teeth, and so on and so on and so on and so on. Seeing through the clutter means being able to focus on what's important. What's *really* important. *And then letting the rest go.*

In order to do this—to let go of what's not important—we have to *figure out* what's important and what isn't. And this is not such an easy thing to do. It takes dedication and practice. Instead of blindly accepting all our thoughts as "truth," we need to examine them one by one. When we find our headspace feeling cluttered, we need to constantly ask ourselves, "Is whatever I'm worrying about *really* important? Does it really matter in terms of my life now and my future happiness?"

Remember when you went through your closet and got rid of all the clothing that didn't fit you now, make you feel fantastic, or wasn't flattering? Similarly, you can deal with your thoughts this way. I don't mean to say that you should try to force yourself to think only about happy things. Difficulty is a part of life. However, your headspace is limited just as your physical space is limited. You don't have room or time for useless stuff that is going to bog you down or trip you up!

THREE COMMON KINDS OF HEADSPACE CLUTTER

❶ JEALOUSY. Jealousy comes in a thousand different flavors, and each one tastes bad! But as pointless and unpleasant as jealousy is, most people experience the feeling at some point. You can be jealous of someone who you think is better-looking than you or has more friends than you; you can be jealous of someone who gets better grades or is better at your favorite sport. You can be jealous of someone whose hair always seems to fall in perfect waves even when it's really humid out, and you can be jealous of someone whose entire life, from the outside, seems perfect. The thing about jealousy is that, like clutter, it is a complete waste of time and energy. Jealousy isn't inspiring; it doesn't make you strive to make your life better. Jealousy is draining, energy-sucking, and misery-making.

Everyone on this planet is different; everyone has different strengths and weaknesses. And no matter how perfect someone else's life may seem, you simply cannot tell what someone else's life is actually like from the outside.

Next time you're feeling jealous of someone, imagine the life *you* want to live, and write down a list of five small steps you can take *right now* to help lead yourself toward the life you want to live. Focus on yourself and your own life. Direct your energy back toward yourself. And then, like a super scratched CD that you can't even listen to anymore, let the jealousy go.

❷ WORRIES ABOUT THE FUTURE. It's natural to want the future to go well, but there is *never* any reason to worry. Why? Because worrying takes up an awful lot of energy but doesn't actually *do* anything for you or your life. Worrying about a test doesn't make you more likely to do well on it. And worrying about your girlfriend breaking up with you doesn't make her more likely to love you forever.

So next time you're worried about something, see if you can channel that worry energy into action! If you're worried about a test, study for it. If you're worried about forgetting your lines in the school play, practice them! If you're worried about getting into college, work really hard on your applications. And if you're worried about something completely outside of your control, then just try to focus on something else. Worrying doesn't prevent bad things from happening; worrying just prevents you from enjoying the moment you're in.

❸ NEGATIVE THOUGHTS ABOUT YOURSELF. Of all the people I've met in my entire life, I cannot think of a single one who was inspired by hearing someone tell them how horrible they are. Even (especially!) if the people telling them how horrible they are, are themselves!

If you want to lose weight, telling yourself "I'm a fat monster" isn't going to make it easier to eat healthily and exercise. And if you really want to do well on a test, telling yourself "I have to study a lot because I'm stupid" isn't going to make it any easier to remember your notes. In fact it's going to make it harder. Hearing negative things about yourself is just going to make you unhappy. And miserable people aren't particularly productive when it comes to getting things done. Next time you start "inspiring" yourself by saying something mean to yourself, try to turn the negative comment into a positive one. Instead of "I'm a fat monster" think, "I'm going to start eating more healthily and exercising more. Good for me!"

I know it sounds incredibly lame and silly. And I know that sometimes friends "bond" over bashing themselves together. But self-bashery is like keeping a bunch of ugly, unflattering clothing in your closet—useless and pointless. Those thoughts just make you feel bad. And they're taking up valuable space in your head!

ONLINE AND OFFLINE GAMES

I'm not here to tell you to abandon the World of Warcraft universe or to give up on your goal of mastering the song "Green Grass and High Tides" on Rock Band. It's great to have a stress reliever and a way to unwind. We all need time for fun. But there's a difference between doing something we actively enjoy and doing something because we're addicted to it. Online and offline games can be lots of fun, but they can also be incredibly addictive and take us away from our actual lives.

And yes, I totally get that sometimes getting away from our actual lives can be not a side effect but the entire *point* of a certain activity. People do lots of things in the name of getting outside of themselves—

adults, teens, kids, everyone—but when getting outside of ourselves becomes the sole purpose of our lives, then we know there's a problem.

Spending too much time playing video games keeps you detached from your actual life and intensely focused on reaching goals in a world that does not actually exist. Completing a quest in a role-playing game might *feel* like a big accomplishment, but as soon as you're no longer in front of the computer, that accomplishment vanishes. It is no match for the feeling of accomplishment you can get reaching goals in your actual life.

Okay, you might say, but so what? It's fun!

Yes, it's true. And I am a huge believer in having fun. If each of us had all the time in the world, then there'd be no reason not to spend a week, a month, a year, or five solid years doing nothing but playing video games. But the problem is that life is short.

Everyone says that, I know. The phrase "life is short" is tossed around so often and in so many contexts that it's easy to forget what that actually means. But what it means is this:

Just as you do not have unlimited space in your backpack, you don't have unlimited time in which to live. Do not fill your life with distractions; do not fill your life with things you only *like*. Fill your life with things, people, and activities that you *love*. Or at the very least things, people, and activities that will help you have the life you want to live. If the life you want to live cannot be complete unless you finish level nine of Halo 3, then by all means go ahead and play it. But if your goals are different from that, you might want to spend more time on those and less on living in a virtual world.

E-maiL/faCeBOOH/MYSPaCe/IM/TWITTeR

Okay, I'm not trying to make myself sound too old here with a back-in-my-day-we-didn't-even-have-phones-if-we-wanted-to-talk-to-a-friend-we-had-to-shout-real-loud story, but the truth is, when I was sixteen, we simply didn't *have* as many ways to stay in touch with friends as teens do today! And having access to so many different types of electronic communication can be both a blessing and a curse. E-mailing, IMing, Facebooking, and Twittering with your friends can be a lot of fun, but one thing being online constantly does is dilute our interactions. Instead of calling our best friend on the phone every night, we're IMing, e-mailing, Facebook messaging, and Tweeting with ten friends at once. And while it can be nice to be in touch with a lot of people at once, it's really a matter of quantity versus quality.

Online communication has its place—it's great for talking to your new online friend who lives in India, or your sister while she's at college three time zones away, but what about your best friend, who lives down the block? Go over and see her while the two of you still live in the same town! Online communication only adds to our lives when we use it in addition to face-to-face (or phone) communications, not instead of it.

TV

There is a difference between watching a few shows that you actually love and turning on the TV and watching it just because it's there and it's easy. We've discussed the idea of paying conscious attention to the items we're bringing into the SWYKS, to not filling up all our space with things we don't actually want or need, and to that same end filling up all of our time with TV shows that we barely even *like* doesn't seem to make a lot of sense. If you look forward to watching a certain show every week, by all means make it a special occasion and watch it every single week. Call your best friend during the commercial breaks, and update like crazy about it on your Twitter account.

But if you find yourself turning on the TV to any random channel to some random show just because you're looking for something to watch, that makes no more sense than going to the store and picking out any shirt that's your size, just so you'll have a full closet.

CLUTTER-FREE FRIENDSHIP TIPS

A lot of things in our lives are not up to us. We can't choose our parents or our siblings; we can't choose our house or where we go to school. But one thing we can choose is our friends. Great friends can make a bad day good and a good day great. But just like every other area of our life, occasionally our friendships can get cluttered with pointless, needless crap. Here are some tips for clearing the clutter:

1 AVOID COMPETITION. A little friendly competition between friends can be fun, so long as it really is friendly. But if you have a competitive streak, it helps to keep it in check as far as friendships are concerned. There is a fine line between a completely jokey battle to see who can get the highest score on Guitar Hero and an actual battle that leaves everyone feeling bad. Competitions— even unspoken ones (*especially* unspoken ones)— over who's smarter, who has more friends, who's better-looking, etc. end with *everyone* as the loser. And by that I mean to say that even if you "win" a competition with a friend, you've lost something in your relationship. First and foremost you should feel like your friends are on your "team," and they should feel like you're on theirs.

2 HAVE REALISTIC EXPECTATIONS. As much as you love your best friend, don't expect him or her to be perfect. There is not a single person on this planet who never makes mistakes. And if there were? Well, that person would be pretty boring to hang out with. Everyone gets snappy sometimes; everyone is a less than perfect friend sometimes; everyone needs time to themselves sometimes. I'm not saying that you should stick with a friend who acts like a jerk—a constantly cranky, snappy, or thoughtless friend deserves to be tossed like a year-old issue of

In Touch. But if you have a great friend who is in a bad mood one day, cut her some slack! Getting annoyed over every tiny thing not only puts strain on a friendship, it puts strain on you, too.

3 BE THE FRIEND YOU WISH YOU HAD. Imagine your ideal friend. What are his or her good qualities? Is this friend always there for you? Does this friend look on the bright side of every situation? Always invite you to do fun stuff? Call to check up on you when you're sick? Great, now instead of going out and trying to find this fabulous person and befriend them, *become* this fabulous friend for someone else. Be the friend you wish you had. This alone is one of the most important ideas to bring with you into any relationship.

4 WHEN YOU'RE THERE, BE THERE. If your best friend is telling you about getting dumped by his girlfriend, you should not be secretly checking your cell phone. And if you're on the phone with your best friend who is telling you about the horrible day she had, don't be sitting in front of the computer checking your e-mail while she's talking. Have you ever been talking to a friend about something important to you, only to hear a quiet *clickety-click-click* in the background and realize he or she has been typing? This is not a good feeling! We're so used to trying to do a bunch of things at once that it can be really tempting to try to multitask our friendships. But you (and your friends) will be happier if you don't!

5 **FIGHT FAIR.** Sometimes even the best of friends will get into a fight. This is inevitable. But when you do fight, make sure you fight fair. Start your fight with this premise: "You're my friend, and I want to figure out how we can make our friendship better." Few fights are completely one-sided. Instead of going into a fight with a friend trying to convince them that they're wrong and you're right, go into the fight trying to better understand their viewpoint.

CLUTTER-FREE ROMANCE

"True love is friendship caught on fire." Have you ever heard this phrase before? It's been making its way around the Internet lately. Some say it's a French proverb. Others say it's by "anonymous." Regardless of the source, this is one of the truest phrases I've ever heard. Many of the happiest romantic relationships have friendship as their base. Yet for some reason, so often in our society we treat friendships and romantic relationships as though they're completely separate things. All of the clutter-free friendship tips completely apply when it comes to decluttering your relationship with a girlfriend or boyfriend.

COMPETING DEMANDS: LESS IS MORE

Our society's obsession with "more = better" doesn't just apply to how we are told to think about our stuff; it applies to how we're told to think about every aspect of our lives. If being involved in one after-school club is good, being involved in five is better; if having three close friends is good, having fifteen close friends is better. We're constantly told we should be in every club, play every sport, go to every party. But there is a fine line between having a full and rich life and having an overstuffed life that's too full to be enjoyed. Surely you've heard the phrase "less is more" before. But what does this really mean? It means that in order to really appreciate anything in your life, you need *room* to appreciate it—mental, physical, and emotional.

Can you really relax and enjoy a party if you know you have to leave in half an hour to go to the next one? And how much can you focus on your basketball game if you know you have to play in a soccer game, a hockey game, and a tennis match right after?

It might sound great to have three hundred best friends—after all, you'd be the most popular person at your school! But would you actually have *time* to have three hundred best friends? Could you really devote energy and attention to each of those friends?

With three hundred friends to attend to, would you even have *time* to be close to a single one?

Sometimes understanding and living the idea of "less is more" might mean giving up one activity so you have time to focus on another one. Only a certain number of shirts will fit into a drawer, and only a certain number of activities will fit into your life. You might want to do everything, but realistically you don't have the time to do everything. So then, how do you choose between the competing demands in every area of your life? Who do you listen to? What are you supposed to do?

You're supposed to imagine the life you want to live. And then listen to your gut. Your life is meant to be enjoyed, but the only person who really knows what you enjoy is *you*.

CHAPTER 14

YOUR SCHOOL LIFE

HOMEWORK

In a perfect world the school day would end when the last period bell rang. But in the actual world it can feel like the moment the bell rings isn't so much the end of school as the start of *homework*. So you have a lot of it, and that sucks. But being disorganized and cluttered makes everything worse. Here are a few tips on getting through a massive pile of homework without going totally nuts.

① ENOUGH WITH THE MULTITASKING! Here in this culture we put so much emphasis on multitasking that we forget that it is only truly possible to really concentrate on one thing at a time. If you have assignments for five classes, you might feel like jumping back and forth between them will make it easier to get it all done. But all it'll do is make it easier for you to *go crazy!* No matter how much you have to do and how many different things you have to do, it is only humanly possible to focus on one assignment at a time. Trying to do more won't make you more productive; it'll just make you feel more cluttered and stressed. So start one project and work on it until it's done. *Then* start on the next one.

2 **MAKE A SCHEDULE.** It might seem silly to make a homework schedule *every night*, but when you're stressed out, having a schedule can be a big help. Before you sit down to do your homework, take just a few minutes to look at everything you have to do and figure out an order that makes sense to do it in. And then write it down. When you're figuring out the order in which to do everything, save the easier or faster assignments for later in the evening and tackle the harder stuff first, when your brain is fresh. Save your favorite subject's homework for last.

3 **CLEAR AN UNCLUTTERED WORKSPACE.** Don't try to do your homework on a messy desk. Although by now

your desk should be clutter-free, make sure it stays that way! Before you begin an assignment, make sure all random objects—extra papers, empty water glasses, and whatever else—have been moved somewhere else. It's a lot easier to concentrate if the only things in your direct line of vision relate to the task you're working on.

4 **ASSEMBLE ALL YOUR MATERIALS BEFORE YOU BEGIN.** You don't want to have to stop an assignment in the middle because you realize you've left the book you need in your backpack, which is out in your car. Assemble everything you need to complete a particular assignment first, before you even begin. If you need to call a friend to ask any homework questions, do this before you begin.

5 **AVOID DISTRACTIONS.** Although there are those who say music helps them concentrate, I must admit I have never been one of those people. If I'm trying to think and listen to music at the same time, I just end up half listening to the music and half concentrating on whatever I'm thinking about and not really paying attention to either. That said, if you're one of those people who truly works better with music on, great. Fine. But don't try to convince me that you can do work just fine in front of the TV. I won't believe you!

6 TAKE BREAKS. For every fifty minutes you work, take a ten-minute break. First, set a timer (an egg timer or the alarm on your cell phone will do) to go off fifty minutes from when you start. Then begin to work. While you're working, don't answer your phone or check your voice mail or your text messages. Don't just take a quick peek at Facebook to see if anything exciting is going on in there. If you tend to think of important things you absolutely "need" to do the moment you sit down to concentrate on something else, keep a pad next to you while you're working, and jot these things down. You can deal with them later. But for the most part, when you're working . . . work! And then, when you've worked for fifty minutes, take a ten-minute break. Get up, stretch, get a snack, write a hilarious text message to your best friend, do some jumping jacks. Do whatever you need to do for ten minutes. But when the ten minutes are up . . . back to work!

Exams

All the homework strategies discussed above can and should also be used when it's exam time. And here are a few more tips:

1 MAKE THE MEMORIZATION PROCESS ACTIVE. When you have to memorize a lot of information, instead of just staring at your notes trying to remember them, *do something*. And by that I mean make flash cards or rewrite all your notes by hand. (In my experience it's easier to remember something you've written by hand than something you've typed on your computer.) Making the process active is much less boring than just staring at a piece of paper for an hour, and if you keep your brain involved in the task, you're probably more likely to actually remember it!

2 **MAKE A STUDY SCHEDULE.** Have you ever had one of those dreams where you go to school in the morning only to find out that your midterm exam is that day and you didn't know and you completely forgot to study? Those dreams are the worst, right? You know what's even worse than that? When it happens in real life! Instead of waiting until exam time to put studying for exams in your homework schedule, write them down as soon as you find out about them, even if the exam is months away. Then figure out how many days you'll need to study, and count backward, writing *STUDY FOR X EXAM* in as part of your homework. Put it on your homework schedule, and schedule it in just like you'd schedule an assignment that was due the next day.

3 **REWARDS.** Look, no one said studying was fun. And sure, a job well done is its own reward and all that and blah blah blah. But let's be honest here—it makes the whole studying process a lot more bearable if you know you have something to look forward to when you're done. So make sure that, no matter how busy you are, you schedule in at least fifteen minutes (if not more) at the end of each day to do something you enjoy—whether it's playing your favorite video game, or calling your best friend, or simply sitting there and doing nothing. Homework is important, and studying is important, but it's also important to make sure that you're enjoying your life, too.

GETTING THE MOST OUT OF YOUR DEVICES

Did you know your iPod has a notes section and a calendar? Did you know your iPod even has an alarm? And that a lot of cell phones have digital recording devices built right in? And a tiny toothbrush folded into the back? (Okay, fine, the last one was a joke.) Well, if you're like most people, the answer is probably no. But using each of your electronics for multiple functions can save you a lot of time, money, and space. Want to learn more? Just go to Google and search for "alternative uses for your [device name goes here]" and I guarantee you tons of stuff will come up that will surprise even the most knowledgeable techie.

ORGANIZING A CLUB AT YOUR SCHOOL

Let's say you love Ping-Pong. You eat, breathe, and sleep Ping-Pong. You wish you could Ping-Pong all day long. But the problem is, your school doesn't have a Ping-Pong club. What do you do? You imagine the life you want to live. And if that involves being in a Ping-Pong club, well, then you start one yourself!

Every school has a different set of rules concerning the forming of new clubs. But here are a few tips that will probably help:

1 MAKE SURE THERE WILL BE PEOPLE TO JOIN YOUR CLUB. If you'd be interested in joining a certain type of club, chances are other people will be interested too. However, it might be good to ask around a little, anyway. First and foremost talk to your friends. If your brand-new underwater juggling club is only going to have two members, you might want to know that ahead of time.

2 THINK ABOUT THE TYPES OF ACTIVITIES YOUR CLUB WILL DO TOGETHER. If it's a Ping-Pong club, you'll probably play Ping-Pong. But you might also go watch a professional Ping-Pong match. If you're starting a humor magazine, you'll probably have meetings to discuss submissions, and you'll probably have other meetings to raise funds to get the magazine printed. If you're starting a fund-raising club to raise money for a particular charity or organization, your club will spend more of its time getting ready for and hosting fund-raising events.

3 FIND A TEACHER OR FACULTY MEMBER WHO WILL SPONSOR YOUR CLUB. Most clubs need an adult to act as "supervisor." Think about any teacher or faculty member whom you particularly like or who you know already has an interest in the topic of your club.

4 THINK ABOUT THE STRUCTURE OF YOUR CLUB. Will there be a president? A vice president? A secretary? How many members would you ideally like to have? How will the offices be appointed?

⑤ FIND A LOCATION FOR YOUR FIRST MEETING. More likely than not this will be somewhere on school grounds. You'll have to check with your school's principal or vice principal to find a spot.

⑥ RECRUIT MEMBERS AND SET A TIME FOR YOUR FIRST MEETING. Think about how you'll let your fellow students know about your brand-new club. Will you put up posters? Hand out flyers? Make an announcement on the morning announcements or put an ad in the school paper?

⑦ HOST YOUR FIRST MEETING. At your first meeting everyone should discuss what he or she is hoping to get out of the club. For example, if you're starting a graphic novels club, are members hoping to write and draw graphic novels, or are they hoping to read and discuss them? It's important that you come to the first meeting with a clear idea of the agenda yet at the same time give everyone who has come to the meeting a chance to talk. If your club is a fund-raising club or is obviously going to need a large budget, this might be a good time to brainstorm some fund-raising ideas. Will you be asking for money from local businesses? Hosting a car wash? A bake sale? A bagel breakfast? A raffle? An auction? A lemonade stand? A quick search on the Internet will reveal hundreds of different ideas and different options.

CHAPTER 15

WHAT TO DO WITH MESSY PARENTS

If all your knowledge about the world were culled from endless hours of TV sitcoms, you'd assume that all teens are messy and all parents are neat. That's the stereotype, anyway. But if you look around you, you'll see that often that's just not true. Far from it! So what are you supposed to do when your parents are the ones leaving the piles of magazines all over the kitchen table? Or if it's their football figurine collection taking up the entire living room? Or what if you're a recent clutter-free convert, but the rest of your family isn't? Now, as a professional organizer I will tell you—you can't force someone to declutter if they don't want to. And even if you could, the mess would come creeping back in no time at all! But while you can't force your family to go clutter-free, there are certain things you can do to help inspire your family to *want* to start getting rid of some of their excess stuff.

Get ready for Operation **TOSSS**.

OPERATION TOSSS

1. **T—TALK TO YOUR FAMILY.** This is the first and most important step to getting them on board for a big decluttering. Just talk to them! Tell them everything that you've learned so far. Tell them

you know that decluttering and cleaning can be a pain, but that your own recent decluttering efforts have changed your way of looking at things. Tell them about how much better, calmer, and happier you feel now that you are clutter-free.

❷ O—OFFER TO HELP. Volunteering to help your family get motivated to declutter might shock your parents and siblings, especially if they're used to seeing you stuck under your own giant pile of clutter. But that's not a bad thing. Shock is your friend. The more shocked they are, the more likely they'll be to take you up on your offer! Besides, knowing that someone will be there with them through the seemingly overwhelming first stages of a decluttering can make the whole thing feel more palatable. Teach your family how to make Space Function Charts, tell them about the Kick Start, and lend them your decluttering playlist.

❸ S—SHOW THEM WHAT YOU'VE DONE. Sometimes the best way to motivate others is to show them by example. If they're still reluctant to embark on their own decluttering, why not give your family a tour of your brand-new decluttered spaces? Show them your closet, your backpack, or your bathroom shelf. If they can see how well your new clutter-free lifestyle is working for you, they'll be more likely to get on board.

4 **S—SET A TIME.** Start small. A lot of families barely have time to sit down to dinner together, let alone time to clean their entire house together. However, even the busiest family can probably devote an hour a week to decluttering together. So set a time to declutter just one area of your home, a time when you think most members of your family will be free. You can't force them to come, but you can let them know that, say, on Sunday from four to five you will be starting to declutter your family room. And that you'd love some help.

5 **S—STRANGE AND SILLY THINGS CAN MAKE IT FUN.** Instead of taking it all so seriously, make the decluttering a fun event for your family. Put up signs all over your house advertising Declutter Day like it's a local festival. Create a soundtrack. Pack a picnic lunch. Make a few awards for the winner of the Decluttering Contest, which you'll be judging. Yes, these ideas are semiridiculous, but if you can convince your family that decluttering doesn't have to be a miserable experience, they're much more likely to want to do it.

FROM KIDHOOD TO ADULTHOOD: HANDLING THE CHANGE

When you were a little kid, it probably seemed like nothing you did really mattered. You could fail a spelling test or eat paste or throw sand, and the worst thing that would happen was you wouldn't get a gold star or you'd get a sticky mouth or you'd have to sit on the bench during recess. Remember what that was like? It was freeing in a certain way, knowing you could kind of do whatever. But at the same time you probably didn't get to make any of your own decisions. Every second of your day was planned out for you.

Now things are different. The great part is that now you're allowed to do more stuff. But the scary part is that now what you do *counts.* The things you say, the choices you make—they have consequences. Not just little tiny consequences that last only through recess, but real-life consequences that last for far longer.

And to suddenly go from no consequences to big consequences is . . . well, it's a lot of pressure! The knowledge of this brings up a lot of questions like:

How can you live in the moment and still plan for the future? How can you deal with knowing that things *do* matter in terms of your future, without going crazy with the stress? How can you figure out what's important, when suddenly *everything* seems important?

These are tricky questions, and there are no easy answers. However, here are some strategies you can adopt to help you clear the mental clutter of too much pressure.

① KEEP THINGS IN PERSPECTIVE. There is a fine line between knowing something matters and thinking the outcome of a particular test, event, or situation will determine *the entire rest of your life.* Getting into college does matter. But not getting into your first-choice school does not mean the rest of your life is shot. No one test, one event, one game, or one play will make or break your whole future. That's just not how life works. So although it might *feel* like a bad grade or a college rejection is the end of the world, the reality is, it's not. When you imagine the life you want to live, know that there are many roads that lead there. Not just one.

② STRIVE FOR BALANCE. Your life should never be all one thing or all the other. A happy existence with minimal mental clutter is most likely found in the in-between areas—when you've found that perfect place between planning ahead and enjoying the now. Owning items you love and enjoy without getting cluttered with extra stuff you don't need. Balancing work and play. Struggling and resting. There is no exact formula for how much of each of these things is the "right" amount. Everyone is different. But when you find yourself feeling out of whack, it can help to look at your life and see which areas are getting too much attention and which areas are getting not enough.

③ REMEMBER THAT WORRYING NEVER SOLVES ANYTHING. We discussed this earlier, but I cannot stress this point enough: *Worrying never solves anything. Doing* solves problems. *Worrying* just makes you miserable. If you have a test, study. If you have college applications to fill out, work on them. If you have a big sports event, practice. Do the best you can in any particular situation, and then relax. Your best is the best you can do.

④ DON'T EXPECT PERFECTION. You are a human, and humans make mistakes. You cannot expect yourself to do everything flawlessly. Making the transition between being a kid and being an adult is a really tough thing to do. There will be bumps along the way. You will do fabulous things, and you will do dumb things too. This is not my opinion, and this is not a guess. This is a fact. Realizing this and accepting it is one of the best ways to clear the mental clutter associated with growing up.

YOUR FAMILY LIFE

FIGHTING, FAMILY-STYLE

All families fight sometimes. Your family, my family, every family on this planet. When you're living in close quarters with other people, some amount of conflict is inevitable. But whether you engage in *Jerry Springer*–worthy screaming matches or calm reasonable discussions is at least in part up to you. Here are some suggestions on how to remove some of the clutter from your fights:

1 **APPROACH FIGHTS FROM A PLACE OF LOVE.** Okay, so you might not always like your younger sister. And sometimes your dad is a big nag. And maybe your mom gets on your nerves. And your younger brother can be a grade-A jerk. Remember, your family is your family, and they're the only one you've got. When you're approaching any member of your family about any issue, large or small, it helps to at least *remind* yourself that even if you don't always like this person, you do love this person (even if you might not always feel like saying it).

2 **FIGHT ABOUT ONE THING AT A TIME.** Don't try to multitask your fights! And don't let your fights get cluttered with bits and pieces of previous fights. Fight about one thing at a time. If you're mad at your brother because he always hogs the shower in

the morning, talk about that. Don't bring up the time he accidentally erased the recording of your favorite TV show. If you find yourself using the phrase "you always" or "you never," this is a pretty strong indication that you're trying to multitask-fight and that it's probably time for a larger discussion. All grievances can and should be discussed, but when you're steaming mad is not the time.

③ REMOVE THE CLUTTER OF UNREALISTIC EXPECTATIONS.

At some point every single person you have a relationship with is going to do something or say something you won't like. And every single person you have a relationship with is going to not like something you say or do. And that's okay! What's not okay is somehow assuming things should be any different. People are who they are, and there is not much you can do to change anyone else. Wishing your family members were different is about as reasonable as wishing your closet would magically grow while you're sleeping—a waste of energy, a waste of time, and a waste of mental space! Do your best to love your family *as they are now.* Maybe one day they will change, and maybe one day they won't. They are only human, just like everyone else.

④ REMOVE THE CLUTTER OF ALWAYS NEEDING TO BE RIGHT.

People will keep a house filled with stuff they do not want because they'd rather hang on to it than face the fact that buying it was a mistake, and people will stay in fights and argue viewpoints they do not even believe in just to avoid admitting they were fighting on the wrong side. Why? Because most people hate to admit when they were wrong. Which is silly, since *everyone* is wrong at some point. Or at many points!

When it comes to decluttering your relationship with your family (or anyone else, for that matter), one of the best things you can do, if not *the* best, is to give up the idea that you always need to be right. So next time you're accusing your younger sis of eating your last ice-cream sandwich, if you suddenly realize that actually *you* ate it *yourself*, there is no shame in saying, "Hey, you know what? I was wrong; you are right. I'm sorry!" In fact, admitting when you're wrong is something to be proud of—it's one of the most adult things a person can do (even though it seems like plenty of adults still haven't learned how to do it).

CHAPTER 16

YOUR FUTURE LIFE

The older you get, the more stuff is up to your own choosing. But with the added freedom will come added responsibility. (I'm sorry if I sound like your parents here, but facts are facts, people!)

JOBS

Bringing your decluttering skills to work with you will not only help you get the job but will help you do it better and more efficiently.

Here are a few jobs teens commonly have to which you can apply your decluttering skills:

BaBYSITTeR

1 **COME PREPARED.** There's nothing worse than spending an entire afternoon with a bunch of little kids who are hopped up on sugar when you have nothing planned to keep them from smearing pudding all over their parents' couch. Make a babysitting kit full of non-mess-making supplies to keep the kids entertained. It'll make your job easier, and their parents will definitely thank you.

Your no-mess babysitting kit can include:

o **PAPER PLATES**—great for making masks, mobiles, and pretend pizzas.

o **ERASABLE COLORED PENCILS.**

o **KID-FRIENDLY SCISSORS.**

o **MAD LIBS**—what kid (or what adult for that matter) doesn't love Mad Libs? To save extra money, try making your own.

o **BOOKS**—it's hard to make a mess with a book. While most families will already have some kid-friendly books in their home, the kids have probably read these already. Picking up a couple of inexpensive books to bring over will make you the best babysitter, and you can reuse them on all the kids you sit for.

? KEEP A BABYSITTING BINDER. If you're regularly babysitting for more than one family, a babysitting organizer can be a great way to keep track of each family's different info. Each family's section in your organizer should contain emergency numbers, their address, the house phone number, and any other pieces of information you'll need to remember, including specific things about each kid. For example, if Little Jessie freaks out without her stuffed hippo, and Little Max starts screaming if you offer him any red foods, it'd help to remember this ahead of time.

BaRISTa/CaFÉ WORKeR

I CLEAN AS YOU GO. If you spill something, mop it up right away. It might seem like you're saving time by leaving a mess for later, but chances are you're not; you're only making more work for yourself or someone else. Liquid messes tend to travel, and that little puddle of espresso you spilled a few minutes ago could quickly turn into a big brown stain on your favorite shirt.

② ESTABLISH ZONES AT WORK. When you're making four different espresso drinks at once, those extra seconds it takes you to find your rag can really add up! If you get used to *always* leaving the chocolate syrup to the right of the grinder, or *always* leaving the milk just to the left of the steamer, it'll make your life a lot easier when you're stressed and in a hurry.

③ MULTITASKING. Okay, remember when I said not to multitask? Well here's one of the few situations in which that advice doesn't apply. If you're the barista and you have a ton of drinks to make, forget everything I said about not multitasking. In certain types of work environments multitasking is not only okay; it's essential!

Server at a Restaurant

① CLEAN AS YOU GO. If this is important when you're a barista, it's *doubly* important when you're working as a server. After all, as a barista chances are you're only expected to move around in ten to fifteen feet of space,

but as a server you have a much bigger space to cover. And that means many more chances for messes, stains, and spills. That seemingly harmless blob of ketchup on the floor won't seem so harmless when you're carrying four bowls of soup and it sends you sliding across the kitchen!

❷ ESTABLISH ZONES AT WORK. Pick a designated spot for a rag, a designated spot for your checks, a designated spot for a pen. And then keep an extra pen too! When you're in a hurry, the last thing you want to be doing is running all over the place looking for an extra pen.

❸ SET A HIERARCHY. Being a server at a restaurant can be a really stressful job. Table three wants a side of ranch dressing, table four needs to place their order, table six hates their food, table nine wants to pay, and you just saw that guy at table one slip the saltshaker into his pocket. Five things need to be done at once, but you can only do one thing at a time. Where do you go first? If you establish a hierarchy of what gets done first, and memorize it, it'll make it a lot easier to figure out what to do next when the pressure is on. Instead of having to make constant snap decisions over what to do next, you'll already *know*. For example, customers waiting for their food will probably fall higher in your hierarchy than dirty plates waiting to be picked up from a table whose customers have already left.

Leaving Home

Chances are, you won't be living with your parents forever. One day you will move out of the home where you grew up. Maybe go off to college. And then, for maybe the first time in your life, there is no one watching over you and telling you what to do. This is super exciting! But it can also be crazy and stressful.

Even the most naturally neat and organized person can find himself cluttering up when it comes time to transfer his entire life to a tiny dorm room or first apartment. Add new roommates, new freedoms, and new responsibilities into the mix, and it's no wonder that the first year of college is cluttery for almost everyone. Surviving the first year away from home can be pretty tricky, college or not. I won't try to squish everything I have to say about this topic into a few short paragraphs, but here are a couple of tips:

Roommates

There's nothing I can say to you to ensure that you'll have a clutter-free relationship with your roommate.

After all, everyone has had a different upbringing and has different ideas of how to live and different thoughts on how a room should look and be. Maybe you have a handle on your clutter situation, but that doesn't mean your new roommate won't want to drag the previous eighteen years of her life with her to school packed up into a twenty-five-piece set of matching pink luggage. The most important things to bring with you to college aren't a minifridge and a shower caddy but an open mind and your clutter-free communication skills. Simply stating your needs to your new roommate doesn't mean your roomie will agree with you, but speaking calmly and rationally will trump yelling and going crazy in every interaction.

(Oh, and definitely bring a pair of flip-flops for the shower. There's gross stuff growing on the floor in there!)

FINDING BALANCE WHEN YOU'RE ON YOUR OWN

The best and the worst thing about being away from home is that, within reason, you can pretty much do whatever you want. For perhaps the first time in your life you won't have a curfew, you won't be expected to be in bed at a certain hour, and if you don't go to class or your job, your parents won't even know. So great, leave home, be free, have fun. But when figuring out what kind of life you want for yourself when you're newly on your own, don't let yourself get too cluttered with the way those who are just starting college or their first full-time job are portrayed in TV shows and in movies. Think about what *you* want. After all, slacking on all your work, staying up until six a.m., and sleeping until four in a pile of cheese curls and someone else's vomit might look fun in the latest college buddy comedy, but in real life that kind of lifestyle is only fun for so long. (Based on my own personal recollections, it's not fun for more than a few days. But hey, that could just be me.)

REDEFINING YOUR VISION: SETTING REALISTIC GOALS

As you get older, your vision for the life you want to live might change. In fact at some point it almost certainly will. What you want out of life when you're fifteen might not be what you want out of life when you're twenty. It can be a hard thing to want something, work hard for it, achieve it, and then find out that what you thought you wanted might not be what you actually want anymore. *And that's okay.* Changing your mind is part of growing up. It's part of being an adult, too. While it helps to keep your vision in mind, make sure the vision you have for yourself is flexible. Give yourself permission to change, and give yourself permission to continue clearing clutter from your vision every step of the way.

GOING GREEN

Clearing the crap and keeping
from buying stuff we neither
want nor need is not only
good for us individually; it's
good for the environment
and good for our planet.
If we all make an effort to
buy less crap, less crap will be manufactured, and
fewer trucks will need to cart the crap from place to
place. Less fossil fuels will be burned, and less toxic
gas will be belched into the air. Less pollution will
clutter our oceans and our air. Fewer tons of stuff
will fill up our landfills. As we make our way into the
future, I suspect more and more people will find that
living clutter-free is not only beneficial when it comes
to having the life we want to live, but also when it
comes to making the planet a place we can continue
to live on for centuries to come.

CONCLUSION

What do you want your life to be about? The choice is up to you. Just as decluttering isn't really about stuff, your *life* isn't really about stuff. Or, if you ask me, it shouldn't be. Stuff doesn't matter. Your stuff can contribute to your joy—your stuff *should* contribute to your joy, in fact—but, ultimately, stuff is disposable. *All* stuff—everything from old socks to giant TVs to fancy cars. Stuff breaks, or gets stained, or goes out of fashion, or you simply grow tired of it. Stuff loses meaning. Stuff never meant anything to begin with.

You know what lasts? Your love for your friends and family. Your belief in yourself as a person. The experiences you've had. And who you are.

Yet, sadly, there are people who base their entire lives around the acquisition of stuff. Lots of people! In our society this is unfortunately not very uncommon at all. There are people who spend most of their energy figuring out how to get the fanciest watch or the hottest handbag. Getting a brand-new thing can provide a momentary dose of happiness, but stuff-induced happiness is like a sugar rush—it comes on fast but fades quickly. And then you just need more.

You know what lasts? The happiness that comes from creating a real life for yourself. The happiness that comes from loving people who love you in return. The happiness that comes from sharing experiences together and appreciating the things in life that actually matter.

I'm not trying to sound preachy here. I want to help people be as happy as they can be. If stuff were the answer, this book wouldn't be about decluttering; it would be about how to get as much stuff as possible!

If you take away just one thing from having read this book, I hope it's not a tip on how to better organize your backpack, and I hope it's not a piece of advice on throwing away clothes you don't wear. No, if you take away just one thing from having read this book, I hope it's the understanding that the life you want to live is within your reach. Just by holding a clear picture of it in your mind—and adjusting it as necessary—you are starting to bring it toward you. You are capable of amazing things. Don't let your clutter hold you back.

(And if you've learned *two* things from this book, I hope the second one is that it's much easier to go toward the life you want to live when you're not rushing around looking for your lost homework, or tripping over a pile of your old shoes.)

When this book began, maybe you were feeling overwhelmed by some aspect of your life, or perhaps even your entire life. "Hey, it's all too much!" is a phrase you might have said to others, to the mirror, or just inside your head. Hopefully, now you know that you yourself are capable of changing your life. You are capable of taking whatever is too much and making it all just right.

As you go forward into your life, here is what I wish for you:

To wake up every morning excited for your day, excited to see what the world has in store for you and what you have in store for the world. Excited to bring your dreams into reality.

I want you to be able to take pleasure in planning the future and remembering the past, knowing you're no longer hiding in one or the other. You can appreciate the objects that you own, but you no longer feel attached to them in a way that is holding you back. The stuff in your life is just . . . stuff. You keep what you use and what you enjoy, and you let the rest go.

There is one reason and one reason only to declutter your room, your bag, your locker, and your life: Being clutter-free will make your life easier and make your life better. Removing clutter will clear the path between you and the life you want to live. You, right there, sitting there reading this book, can have the life you want. No matter where you're starting from. No matter how big a distance there is between the life you have now and the life you want. You can get yourself there, and all it takes to get started is one single step in the right direction. And it's a lot easier to know which direction is the right direction if you're not stepping forward into clutter.

Imagine the life you want to live. Now go out and make it happen!

THE LIFE YOU WANT TO LIVE!